Healing Pathways

A Journey Through Life's Challenges

Mindy Wiesenberg

Cover design by Natalie Friedemann-Weinberg
Set in Arno Pro by Raphaël Freeman MISTD, Renana Typesetting

ISBN: 979-8-5734-0333-5

This book is dedicated in loving memory of my husband

Johnny Wiesenberg z"l

A devoted husband, father, grandfather and son
who brought love and laughter into our lives.
He lived with memorable values and left us with valuable memories.

🌿

And my parents

Zeev & Paula Racker z"l

Who, through their love, care and devotion laid the roots
that built their everlasting legacy – 'The Racker Clan'

MAY ALL THEIR MEMORIES BE FOR A BLESSING

Your story is going in an unexpected direction; You have received a call to shine light on those pockets of suffering you would have never paid attention to before. It is a rude awakening, and sometimes you may wish to rewind the movie to your life before, or at least fast-forward to the future scene of total healing or remission. That would be nice. But you might miss the grace of the journey, the gifts along the way.

Jeff Foster, *The Way of Rest*

Contents

With Gratitude

'At times our own light goes out and is rekindled by a spark from another person. Each of us has cause to think with great gratitude of those who lighted the flame within us.'

— ALBERT SCHWEITZER

This section is usually titled 'acknowledgements' and can often be found at the back of a book. However, for me, showing gratitude is a fundamental part of any healing journey – and therefore is the starting point of my story.

In Judaism, before carrying out any *mitzvah*,[1] one makes a *brachah*.[2] In this way, we thank God for our ability to be able to perform this good deed and for the blessing that this act bestows upon us. And so, before you begin reading, I want to thank those who have helped to bring this book to fruition, for without them, you would not be holding it in your hands now. I also want to thank all of you who travelled with me on the journey through my challenges, showing me care and support, and helping me to traverse the pathways that have allowed me to heal. Every one of you has been a blessing in my life.

The seed for this book was planted after I was diagnosed with cancer, when I started to write short notes as a sort of diary about my feelings going through treatment. However, it was only some

---

1. Positive commandment.
2. Blessing.

years later, after the sudden death of my husband, Johnny, that the idea of collecting my thoughts into a book took shape. After looking through my diary entries, and creating a structure for them, I shared the idea for this book with my friend, Ann Rosen, with whom I worked on a project that our family was sponsoring in Johnny's memory. Having read some of my writing, she urged me to turn this idea into reality and I thank her for her encouragement.

Members of my family, including my sisters, came up with helpful suggestions after reading the initial manuscript. My daughter Tanya with her analytical and philosophical mind helped me refine many of my ideas into a coherent framework and my daughter-in-law Lianna used her strategic talents to help me develop some key issues, including the cover design. My editor, Sorelle Weinstein, worked her magic on the language and other editorial issues. Natalie Friedemann-Weinberg created the beautiful cover for the book and the internal graphics. Raphaël Freeman used his typesetting skills in creating the layout of the book and gave me advice on publishing.

My deepest thanks go to all the medical teams in the Royal Marsden Hospital and University College Hospital in London and the Moffitt Cancer Centre in Tampa, Florida, without whom I would not be alive today to tell my tale. The doctors, nurses and countless members of staff who looked after me could not have been more professional, compassionate and caring, and so many of them left a deep impression on me. I also thank the many therapists at the Chai Cancer Centre in London who treated me over the years and helped me keep going.

I give thanks too to some people who will probably never even read this book, yet I feel I owe them an enormous amount of gratitude. It was their books that often guided me and have been an integral part of my journey: the numerous authors who are either quoted in my book or referred to in the bibliography. Their ideas and practical strategies have deepened my understanding of so many different aspects of healing and brought me to where I am today.

To my nearest and dearest: I want to thank all my family who have been like friends and friends who have been like family – not just through my illness and bereavement but in many other chapters in my life. You all know who you are and how you have supported me. In particular, I want to thank my sisters Zena and Dina, their husbands John and Harry, and all their children and grandchildren. They are the pillars that support me and the glue that holds me together, as their ongoing love and concern know no bounds.

And finally, to my incredible children – those to whom I gave birth and those who by marriage have become like my own. Tanya and Ian, Avi and Chanie, Natan and Lianna, and Baruch. They have given me more than words can ever express and have added a special beautiful dimension to my life through their children, my adorable grandchildren. They have kept me going through every challenge I have faced and went to extraordinary lengths to be by my side every step of the way. They lifted me up and gave me hope, lighting the path for me to walk along as I healed. They are the reason to carry on my journey.

ALL PROFITS FROM THE SALE OF THIS BOOK ARE
BEING DONATED TO BRITISH EMUNAH.

This charity cares for over 10,000 children and their families in Israel through a network of kindergartens, day care centres, therapy centres, special schools and children's homes. Many of those in their care are disadvantaged or at risk, having suffered abuse and neglect.

For more information about the charity,
visit www.emunah.org.uk and www.worldemunah.org

Preface
A Post-Corona World

'Life is a succession of lessons which must be lived to be understood.'
— HELEN KELLER

I was almost halfway through writing this book in March 2020 when the Coronavirus pandemic struck, a virus that is thought to have originated in China. Paradoxically, the word 'crisis' is written as an ideogram in Chinese that represents the combination of two ideas: 'danger' and 'opportunity'. In many ways, these two concepts sum up how you need to deal with any challenge in your life. A crisis can present a danger or the loss of something or someone dear. But it also presents an opportunity for self-reflection, growth, perspective, gratitude and so much more.

As country after country went into lockdown, and millions were forced to adjust to the new reality of self-isolation, I was struck with the realisation that I was no stranger to self-isolation. During my eight-year cancer journey, there were many times when I needed to self-isolate in order to avoid catching infections while undergoing chemotherapy treatment. I couldn't have any physical contact with anyone: no hand shaking, hugs or kisses, and certainly no travelling on public transport. So, when it came to lockdown, I had already, as the saying goes, been there, done that, and got the T-shirt. For the first time in eight years, I was ahead of the game.

Instead of being the one who had missed out on so much over the years because of my illness, I was now the one ready and prepared to meet this challenge head on, in a way that so many others were not. And I understood that so much of what I had been writing about over the years was now bearing fruit.

When the pandemic struck, my sisters and I realised that we would not be able to travel to visit our children and grandchildren in Israel. We decided to turn this crisis into an opportunity – a virtual opportunity to connect with our family thousands of miles away and do something useful not just for our children but for our grandchildren, too. So, with the help of Zoom, we set up a grandma school, with each of us teaching the whole family a speciality subject once a day. That meant that not only did we get to engage with our grandchildren, but their tired parents got a well-deserved break. As my daughter so aptly quoted, 'When life gives you lemons, learn to make lemonade.' I have been making a lot of lemonade in recent years. I have experienced not just medical crises with my cancer diagnosis, but mental and emotional crises too with a deeper loss in my life – the sudden and unexpected death of my husband. In both these challenges, I had faced the 'danger' but also tried to see the 'opportunities' to heal.

There was another silver lining to the pandemic. I was extremely fortunate that I did not have to worry about loss of employment or income or have a house filled with family to take care of. I was by myself in my own home, self-isolating, and rather than feeling bored and lonely, I had a project to complete: this book. My creativity had been given free rein, and I threw myself completely into my writing. Yet the Coronavirus outbreak had inspired so many to write about isolation as an opportunity for self-realisation. Did I, in my writing, really have anything else to add to the conversation? Still, I realised that I had to complete my task. People were going to be asking themselves some difficult questions, as the patterns of their lives had been disrupted – for some, irrevocably. For years I had invested in looking at ways of healing, and now more than ever, during this global crisis, people needed to heal – and it is not a process that can be achieved overnight. How often do we hear the expression, 'time heals'? But it isn't actually time that heals, but rather what you do with your time. My life had changed unrecognisably over the last eight years, and during my process of healing, I came to the realisation that the methods that had helped me to heal could also help others.

I also realised that even though my journey was a personal one, it had a universal message. We are all living with fear of the unknown, uncertainty about the future, wondering if and how life is ever going to return to normal. Even once restrictions are eased, what exactly is going to be the new 'normal' and what will it mean for our future? Will the gift of time we were given during self-isolation have any enduring benefits?

These are questions which will be answerable only in the fullness of time. In the meantime I invite you to take a journey with me along the pathways I have travelled through the challenges of serious illness and bereavement, and how I have tried to heal myself physically, mentally and emotionally. It is a journey that so many of us take in different ways through the different challenges that we face. Some may face challenges with relationships or finances while others suffer upheaval due to their work or crises of faith. Expectations may not be realised and disappointment follows. Our stories may all be different, but everyone has the ability to heal in their own way.

Introduction
A Wakeup Call

'Knowing yourself is the beginning of all wisdom.'
— ARISTOTLE

There can be a time in your life when an event happens that can change everything. It is often referred to as a wakeup call or lifeshock. Something so paradigm-shifting that you begin to question the solid ground on which you walk. It makes you reassess everything you took for granted before the event, as you realise that nothing will ever be the same again.

In the past eight years I have had two such defining moments, wakeup calls that altered the whole direction of my life. The first was my cancer diagnosis in January 2012 and the second was my husband's sudden, untimely death in January 2018. These events forced me to try to understand so many things about my life and my relationships.

I would not have chosen to come to such a deep sense of self-realisation through such means; believe me, if I could turn the clock back I would, without a second thought. There I would be with my husband by my side, both of us in good health, enjoying our golden years together, living out our retirement near our children and grandchildren. But it was not to be, and the challenges I faced and continue to face needed to be overcome. I had to move forward by cultivating a form of resilience which comes through changing one's mindset. I had to develop a deep understanding of the things that bring meaning to my life and how I can best live that life in the time I have left.

The diagnosis of a serious illness and the death of a loved one were both lifeshocks. Over twenty-eight years ago I suffered another traumatic experience when my father, Zeev Racker, died, also quite unexpectedly and suddenly at the age of sixty-seven. At the time I was a thirty-five-year-old mother with four young children, studying for a master's degree. My life was so hectic that despite the shock and immense feeling of sorrow, I just did not have the capacity or emotional maturity to deal with my father's death in a way that made me reframe my perspective as I did so many years later.

Bereavement and illness are two types of trauma that can create a fracture in your life. In some cases, a trauma can create a fracture that will leave you with a broken heart; in others it can leave you with a broken body. Both these types of fractures need healing. For years, I thought that healing referred only to medical interventions, when things went wrong physically with the body. Since my lifeshocks, I have come to understand that healing is so much more; it is the restoration to full health of any organism so that it can function in its optimum state. Exploring the many ways that healing occurs on a physical, mental and emotional level helped me see that it works in different ways for different people.

They say that there is no one way to finding God, and so it is with building resilience and allowing oneself to heal. Each person finds the path that works for them, finds new ways to grow, in order to become resilient and to heal.

I can only tell you what has worked for me.

There is an ancient Greek expression, 'we suffer our way to wisdom.' I am not sure that I am wiser now than I was before my recent traumas but suffering needs acknowledgement both from the sufferers themselves and from those around them. This acknowledgement is not easy for it opens you up to the realisation that you are vulnerable and will need courage to move forward. Some people are not ready or willing to accept their vulnerability and this too must be acknowledged. But for me, my vulnerability was an essential part of the healing process, which I had to work through. The experience imparted its own wisdom, since allowing yourself to be vulnerable in front of others cultivates strength.

I am not a trained therapist or any type of religious or spiritual teacher. I am just a person who has tried to deal with life challenges, and consequently the grief in its many forms that often results from such hardships. This book is about my journey. It is not a geographical journey for I reside today in a house that is only a ten-minute walk from the house I grew up in. You do not have to travel great distances to make sense of the world around you, for that understanding can often come from an internal journey.

A cancer diagnosis, dealing with the challenges of ill health, and then later a sudden bereavement, have all helped me reframe my view of the world. My situation caused me to contemplate my life. I understood that in order to move forward I had to heal myself; I had to search everywhere I could for what would heal my body and my soul both in the physical sense through the latest medical research and in the spiritual sense through exploring what could nourish my soul.

My family and I spent many hours researching all the latest treatments for my lymphoma and the various trials being undertaken all over the world. I read an enormous amount. Books about healing through diet and exercise. Books about the latest breakthroughs in epigenetics, quantum physics and other scientific fields. Autobiographies of people who had endured significant trauma as well as religious texts and books about the meaning of life – all of which gave me inspiration for how to heal my psyche and soul. The abundance of perspectives found in these books expanded my knowledge of the mind-body relationship, and what it means to heal. My eyes were opened to the benefits of changing your thought patterns and behaviour in order to boost your immune system. I don't think that without the challenges I faced I would have explored all these areas of healing with such a vested interest.

This book is the result of my exploration.

Everyone has a story

They say that everyone has a book inside them and indeed there were many times in my life, especially in recent years, when I wanted to write a book. Yet I came to a love of books late in life. Despite having some wonderful teachers in primary school, I was never a big reader in my early years. My English teacher in secondary school was not very inspiring and I did not enjoy many of the set texts we were taught – with the exception of Romeo and Juliet. Teenage love spoke to me perhaps more than Roman emperors and English kings, but I did develop a fascination with science fiction in my teenage years. When I started university and was encouraged to read widely around my subject of geography, my love for nonfiction began to take root. To this day, I prefer nonfiction and autobiographies to fiction, and having written many academic papers during my degree courses which required copious research, my writing skills were honed in the world of nonfiction.

However, after my father died, I started going to creative writing classes. I needed some way of expressing my grief and thought that by writing about him and his life story, it would help me deal with the vacuum in my life that his passing left. But with time, I realised that the vacuum did not just exist because he was no longer in my life; the vacuum was there because I knew so little about his life. As a Holocaust survivor whose entire family was murdered by the Nazis, he remained a closed book for most of his life, unable to talk about his past, especially to his children, who he wanted to protect from the horrors he had endured. I never did manage to write more than a few essays and so the book remained unwritten.

Many years later, I thought about writing the ultimate wedding planner's guide. After planning my daughter's wedding, I was well versed in all aspects of organising a wedding and felt suitably qualified to write such a book. Of course, that didn't happen either as life took over and inevitably the idea stayed in my head despite the thick file of notes accrued throughout the planning process.

A novel was my next big idea as I decided to return to creative writing classes. I still had this deep yearning to write a story about the Holocaust based on my father's life in pre-war Poland. Although I knew very few specifics of his life, I had read widely around the subject and wanted to craft a story about a family torn apart by the war.

However, that was not meant to be either. Soon after my cancer diagnosis and the eventual start of treatment, I abandoned my creative writing classes. I no longer had the appetite for fiction as my reality became a more complex story in itself. Yet that creative streak within me could not be quashed and I felt that if my time was running out, I wanted to record my life story for my grandchildren, primarily because I felt that the world I grew up in was so different to the world they occupy, and it would be a fun exercise to resurrect my childhood memories. My idea was to combine my own story with that of the growth of the North West London Jewish community, highlighting the history of the schools and communal institutions which had featured in my life. *Memoir of a Hendon Maidel* never exceeded more than 10,000 words tapped out on my laptop. The reason for this was that I was simultaneously undertaking another type of writing, my cancer blog which I began after my diagnosis, and this was far more therapeutic and real in a sense than my memories. It also served as a form of therapy, as I openly expressed my feelings about my illness.

My thoughts had plenty of time and opportunity to wander as I would spend endless hours waiting for hospital appointments and sitting through difficult treatments. I began to record them all. I started to share some of these thoughts with family and friends through emails, and the feedback I received made me realise that my cancer diary would be a more authentic and raw account of my life than any planned memoir. Somehow, I couldn't capture reality looking back at my childhood in the same way as I did with these thoughts. Living with cancer and very difficult treatments made me view life through a different prism. My perspective changed as did my relationships with family, friends and my Creator. In some cases, my relationships intensified. In others, it became clear to me which friendships were meaningful and which were not.

And then, unbeknownst to me, another lifeshock was waiting for me. My husband Johnny's sudden and unexpected death was so deep a blow that the repercussions for all our family were immense.

How did we cope? I honestly don't know – and in part that is what this book is all about. My journey through grief and coping with the loss of my husband could have been a book in itself, as could the story of my cancer journey. But I felt that there was a much deeper journey to record: that of my healing and trying to find wholeness and inner peace, as my message centres around self-awareness and building resilience. I felt that by sharing my experiences and the paths I took to heal, others might draw comfort and inspiration when dealing with their own losses, illness and grief.

Everyone is a story

I have learnt that not only does everyone have a story, but everyone is a story. In life you need to know your own story in order to know who you are and your place in this world. It is what renowned neurologist Oliver Sacks writes in his book The Man who Mistook his Wife for a Hat.

> 'If we wish to know about a man, we ask "what is his story – his real, innermost story?" For each of us is a biography, a story. Each of us is a singular narrative, which is constructed, continually, unconsciously, by, through, and in us – through our perceptions, our feelings, our thoughts, our actions; and not least, our discourse, our spoken narrations. Biologically, physiologically, we are not so different from each other; historically, as narratives – we are each of us unique.

To be ourselves we must have ourselves – possess, if need be repossess, our life stories. We must "recollect" ourselves, recollect the inner drama, the narrative, of ourselves. A man *needs* such a narrative, a continuous inner narrative, to maintain his identity, his self.'

Yet very often, our perception of a situation differs from how others see it. When my sisters read the first draft of this manuscript, they didn't agree with certain things I had written about our upbringing. They remembered things differently. This was exactly what happened when my aunt Susi, my mother's sister, published her life story. My mother, Paula Racker, read the first draft and commented to her that she didn't remember a certain event happening in the way my aunt described. My aunt immediately replied, saying: 'Paula, these are my memories not yours!' So yes, memory is subjective and there will be things I have written which not everyone will remember in the same way; but it is my perspective that has nurtured the image I have had of myself throughout my life.

I have learnt that so much of what heals you is coming to the understanding that, not only does the story of your life change over time, but sometimes the story you believed about yourself throughout your life is not always the genuine one; it is discovering that you have control over your own story that can help you to understand and know your true self. There are so many lessons that life teaches you and through them you can learn who you truly are and what your story is.

What is a 'lesson'? As I see it, a lesson is an experience or fact you have taken from the external environment and internalised. Through this internalisation, a transformation can take place, whether it is in your thought processes, your physical responses or your emotional state. In turn, this transformation will allow you to externalise it to your behaviour and beliefs; it allows you to grow and heal by creating a new reality. Much of what I have experienced through my challenges has taught me that I often failed to internalise many issues in the beginning. It was only through opening my heart and my mind to new ideas and new experiences that I began to internalise things, which transformed my thinking and my physical wellbeing, helping to create a better reality for myself.

This book is about the lessons I have learnt and the paths I have traversed on this healing journey. A lesson can be learning from a particular situation and applying it to a universal one. Each chapter represents a different pathway that guided me along the way. At the end of each one I list the lessons I learnt through my experiences which became my stepping stones on my healing journey. I hope that my story of healing will in some small way touch those of you going through your own challenges so that you, in turn, will be able to apply the lessons to your own situation.

My novel still waits to be written, but then what is fiction if not a collection of one person's ideas, imagined or otherwise?

Pathway One
Finding Wellness within Illness

'The part can never be well unless the whole is well.'

— PLATO

When does the fact that you have cancer actually sink in? When do you turn from a statistic into a patient? When? Does it begin when the doctor says, 'I am not happy with something in your blood tests and I am going to refer you to a specialist'? Does the realisation hit you when you hear: 'I think the results show that it could be a form of lymphoma, but we will need to do further tests'? Or does it take until days after the latest appointment when you are sitting alone at home, after having googled twenty different articles about the supposed type of cancer the doctor says it is? In my case it was none of the above, even though I went through all of those stages. The realisation hit me like a speeding truck after the most mundane event. I had gone out one evening to a meeting without Johnny, and, running late, I had left the kitchen in total disarray. I returned a few hours later to find it in pristine condition. For those of you who know my husband and his distinctly undomesticated habits, this was completely out of character for him and became a turning point. I walked in, took one look at my

1

> transformed kitchen, and burst into tears. It had finally sunk in. I really must be ill. Yes, I have cancer and the message Johnny gave me that night was we are going to deal with this together.

The story of my journey since my cancer diagnosis in 2012, and the subsequent treatments I underwent, could take up a book by itself. It has been an eight-year-long convoluted voyage through seemingly endless doctors' consultations, investigations and tests, hospital admissions, countless chemotherapy treatments, a stem cell transplant and a two-month sojourn in America to undergo a new groundbreaking treatment called CAR-T cell therapy. All of which have left me a different person to the one that began this journey years ago, and that is not just in the physical sense of what my body has had to endure. It is what has happened to my mental and emotional wellbeing that perhaps has created the biggest change in me. I have discovered that in order to heal, it isn't just about learning how to survive but more importantly how to thrive. It is about finding wellness within illness.

The human body knows innately how to heal itself. Its immune system is designed to do precisely this. If you cut your hand or break a bone, once the injury is dressed or bound, the body takes over to repair the damage. Provided no infection spreads, it does not need any other intervention. This is all well and good if you have a fully functioning immune system, but problems arise when the immune system is not working properly, or is overrun with disease, as a result of different factors.

What does it mean to be well?

In the West, to be 'well' is understood as being free from illness and disease. Yet even the World Health Organisation (WHO) defines wellness as 'a state of complete physical, mental and social wellbeing and not merely the absence of disease or infirmity.' The root of the word wellness is 'well' and if you stop to think about it, what is a well? It is a deep hole that has been dug in order to reach a source of water buried below the ground, a source of water that sustains life. In order to attain a state of wellness, you often have to dig deep within yourself to find your vital source of energy, the life force that sustains you. Within the illnesses that you or I might experience is a source of energy that can heal us and sustain us. We have to open ourselves up to the possibility of finding that place and understand just how we can reach it.

Much of the focus in modern medicine is on curing disease and treating its physical symptoms. This is all well and good when the medical intervention is successful, and that is the end of the story. But for many, conventional medical treatment does not cure the illness, as physical and emotional symptoms can still persist.

Perhaps what many in the medical world do not appreciate is that disease in the body really means that the body is suffering from 'dis-ease'. It is not at ease or at peace with itself and the imbalances are not just physical. Our physical wellbeing is deeply interconnected with our mental, emotional and spiritual wellbeing. So when a person is not well, it is not just a question of healing that person physically, but also their lack of ease, for it is this that can contribute to a person's maladies and the symptoms that are manifested.

New paradigm for healing

A distinction needs to be made between being cured of a disease and being healed of a disease. Healing does not necessarily mean you will be cured. You may never recover in the physical sense; you may even die from the disease. But what true healing can do is show you a way that your disease can help you to become whole, to come to a place where your mind, body and soul are in unison, allowing you to know and understand what you really want in life and help you make the choices that will guide you on that pathway. Reaching this place in most cases brings an inner peace in and of itself, and much of this comes when you find meaning in your life and the meaning of your life.

The diagnosis of an illness, whether chronic or acute, can act as a wakeup call to take stock of your life and try to understand what your true purpose is in this world. It is an event outside of you, a shock that requires internalisation for transformation to take place. It is personal to you and if you are blessed to have an external support system that can help you, then that is an added bonus. But even without the aid of family and friends, or financial support, this transformation can still happen. It is your will and attitude that will determine your journey. It is your ability to see a silver lining in the cloud that will alter your perspective. The thought of a possible death sentence hanging over you can cause you to refocus, recalibrate and realign yourself to your deepest values, allowing you to regain a true sense of self and your integrity. I am not sure if at the time of my diagnosis, I was aware that this transformation was taking place inside me, but as the years passed and my cancer journey progressed, I saw this to be the case.

When I was first told that I had cancer, the consultant informed me that it was a very indolent, nonaggressive type of non-Hodgkin lymphoma called Chronic Lymphocytic Lymphoma, or CLL as it is known in the medical profession. In most cases, there is no initial treatment as many patients are put on a 'watch and wait' regime. This basically means you have regular blood tests to check your levels and see when you might need to start treatment if your white cell count rises too high. The shock of the diagnosis was later cushioned by the fact that after researching many articles on CLL and contacting patient support groups, I discovered that it was a very treatable disease without too many serious side effects and people could live until old age with it. This gave me some sense of security, but whether this was false or not at the time didn't matter, as I had been given breathing space. Perhaps that is why it took a while for the reality of my cancer diagnosis to sink in. Other than some mild fatigue, I didn't have any symptoms and I was carrying on with my life as before, as no one knew I was ill.

My husband Johnny and I had made the decision not to tell anyone other than our children, because, at the time, I did not require any treatment. This decision was also made in light of the fact that at the same time that I was diagnosed, my sister Zena received the news that one of her daughters had been diagnosed with cancer. She had endured several cases of cancer in members of her family, and although they were all now clear, I did not want my diagnosis to drain her precious emotional resources.

My initial diagnosis, however, proved to be wrong and after changing consultants and having my spleen removed, as it was the main site of the disease, the doctors diagnosed a different type of rare non-Hodgkin lymphoma called Splenic Marginal Zone, which was also slow-growing and nonaggressive. In the beginning we followed whatever the doctors suggested regarding treatment without thinking too deeply about any other approaches. When I think about it now, my acceptance of this at the time was quite astonishing, as in past years I had been one of those people who had leant towards more alternative and complimentary approaches to health issues. Perhaps it was the overwhelming nature of dealing with a cancer diagnosis, something so out of my normal realm of experience, that forced me into a medical box out of which I could not see any alternatives.

I had been through two operations as a child and had suffered from back pain for many years following an accident at age 18 while working on a kibbutz. At that time, like most people, I considered healing to mean curing something that is wrong with the body and treating its symptoms – whether through a doctor or in the hospital. However, just over twenty-five years ago, when I was in my late thirties, I began to consider alternative medicine like homeopathy and acupuncture, as I found myself suffering from some niggling chronic ailments.

A friend at that time recommended that I read a book by Dr Andrew Weil called *Spontaneous Healing: How to Discover and Enhance Your Body's Natural Ability to Maintain and Heal Itself*. It was a revelation for me. Dr Weil is a world-renowned pioneer in the field of holistic medicine, a healing-oriented approach to healthcare that encompasses mind, body and spirit. His book covers everything from case studies, advice on nutrition and exercise, and dealing with doctors to your mental attitude and ridding your body of toxins. Reading the book was one thing, but putting it into practice was another, and I didn't manage to follow all his recommendations. But what the book did do was open my eyes to the possibilities out there and I took up some of his suggestions. But that's just it...I saw them as suggestions rather than a way of life. Dr Weil's approach is that the body has an innate ability to heal itself; it just needs the right environment both internally and externally to do so.

The concepts I read about in his book lay dormant within me, and I think my inability to reconnect to these ideas in the early days of my cancer diagnosis was, perhaps, because I had associated his holistic approach with chronic nonserious illnesses. After all, that was my frame of reference in the past. My cancer diagnosis was so overwhelming and potentially life-threatening that I wasn't able to consider a different route at the time.

It was only two years into my cancer journey, when I had completed my first set of chemotherapy treatments, that one of my best friends gave me *The Cancer Whisperer* by Sophie Sabbage, a book that would change my entire outlook and approach to my cancer. Sophie Sabbage was diagnosed with stage four lung cancer and was given six months to live. As I write these words, six years later, she is still alive and has become one of the foremost voices in favour of a holistic, integrated approach to treating cancer using both the latest medical treatments combined with complimentary therapies. In essence, her book is about learning how to take back control of your life when everything seems to be falling apart.

Her entire premise is that you do not have to cure yourself from cancer; you have to allow cancer to cure and heal you. With the callout, 'I have cancer. Cancer does not have me,' the book details how you can learn to understand yourself, your disease, its possible causes and all forms of treatment that can improve your wellbeing as you go through illness. It is about finding wellness in illness through learning how to allow your body to heal, and dealing with disease from every perspective, physical, mental, emotional and spiritual.

This book proved to be a turning point in my journey to wellness. It helped me understand how many things in my life had been causing my body stress. It also gave me many practical tips on diet, exercise, and every type of complimentary healing technique, from reiki to acupuncture to detoxing regimes. I tried many of the different therapies including meditation, which for me has been the most used and useful in my life. However, most importantly, the book provided me with guidelines and pathways to follow that would promote my own healing; it allowed me to regain some form of control since cancer intruded into my life. As my cancer journey progressed, and I realised that I was entirely in the hands of my medical teams, gaining back even a small modicum of control in my life was invaluable for my mental wellbeing.

Over time I adapted many strategies in this valuable book to suit me. And that to me is the principal takeaway from my experience: not everything you read, see or hear is suitable or practicable for you. There is no one, ideal route to healing. You have to take in the information and process it through the filter of your own life and evaluate how suitable and manageable it is for you. What's most important is to be open to suggestions and not block off any avenues. Through reading *The Cancer Whisperer*, I began to understand that it was possible to combine the medical treatments that my doctors were recommending with complimentary therapies.

East versus West: different approaches to healing

At this point I think it would be useful to clarify some of the different medical approaches as words like conventional, complimentary, alternative, traditional, holistic and integrative all have different meanings.

The medical approach that most people are familiar with is conventional Western medicine, which is practised in all hospitals in the Western world by doctors who are qualified in different fields. It is the medicine that is responsible for saving millions of lives and takes up most of the healthcare and medical research budgets of nearly all Western countries.

Alternative medicine refers to nonmainstream medicine that is not normally part of standard care for a patient, and includes practices such as homeopathy, acupuncture, chiropractic, herbal infusions, special diets and the like. Many of these practices stem from traditional Eastern medicine and can, in some cases, be used in place of conventional medication. However, there has not been as much scientific research undertaken into the efficacy of some of these treatments as there has been with conventional medicine, even though many therapies have been successful in treating chronic medical conditions.

Complimentary and integrative medicine, on the other hand, are when various types of alternative practices are used in conjunction with conventional medicine. It is not 'either or', but rather a fusion of both traditional Western medicine and alternative treatments.

Holistic medicine is very similar to integrative medicine, except the combining of alternative treatments is usually administered by a single doctor overseeing both conventional and alternative treatments to enhance the health of the patient. The whole person is viewed as one system where the mind, body and spirit are interdependent, and combining both conventional and alternative therapies is seen to create the correct balance within the body.

Whatever route you decide to take in navigating your own medical issue, it's vital that you inform the medical team treating you. They may not agree with some of the alternative methods, but they need to know if you are using them. I heard the story of a cancer patient who decided to go off on his own path with alternative treatments without informing his doctors. They then discovered that some severe reactions he was suffering from were due to various herbal treatments he was taking, which negatively interacted with his chemotherapy.

The integrative approach is the one I undertook for myself as I learnt more and more about how integrating Western and Eastern medicine could have beneficial effects. This was all part of what became my 'health project'. I realised that in order to heal myself, I had to approach my cancer in the same way I had done with other projects, and that was to invest time and energy into creating the best outcome. Sophie Sabbage had outlined many of the ways she had achieved this in her book, using both traditional medicine and complimentary therapies. I have a background in teaching, and am a fairly organised person, but it wasn't until I spoke to one of my doctors that I realised that I needed to embark on my own health project. He advised that I print out every single piece of information – from test results to doctors' letters – and keep them in a file. This suggestion was to prove invaluable, especially when I needed to cross-reference things and later contact hospitals in America. I had compiled my own full medical CV and was able to access my notes without needing to rely on any doctor. Furthermore, when researching any suggested treatments, I printed out facts about them so I could prepare questions for the doctors at the next appointment. I had to educate myself about my illness and all the available treatments by having an open mind and an open heart.

Open mind

Having an open mind is, as I have learnt, what some in the medical profession do not always possess. I know that I was blessed to have some of the best doctors in their fields looking after me throughout my cancer journey, and you could not find more dedicated, caring people. However, the increasing level of specialisation in each area of the body within the medical system has meant that many doctors do not approach or treat the whole body as one system. One may argue that hospital multidisciplinary team meetings were set up precisely for this reason, but these were usually for the purpose of examining physical symptoms in one area of the body, rather than the functioning of the mind and body together. Eastern medicine approaches the mind and the body as part of one system; so many of the ideas behind complimentary therapies and holistic medicine have come from Chinese, Indian and other Eastern medical traditions.

Obviously, one cannot dismiss the huge advances that Western medicine has brought to the world, from vaccinations and antibiotics, X-rays, MRI and CT scans, to organ replacements and cures for cancer. Countless millions of lives have been saved and enhanced by these discoveries, including my own. Had I not been able to access the incredible new treatments for cancer I don't think I would be alive today, even though I kept on having setbacks when the cancer returned. From chemotherapy to the new immunotherapy drugs to the whole process of undergoing a stem cell transplant, each stage depended on the medical and scientific expertise of my wonderful teams. Indeed, the seemingly impossible task of finding a matching donor for my transplant could not have taken place without the modern technology available, and I was incredibly fortunate to find a full matching donor within a very short time. In the UK we are blessed to have one of the most exceptional healthcare systems in the world. The NHS, our National Health Service, delivers world-class expertise and up-to-date treatments at no cost to the patient, a luxury many people around the world can only dream about.

But I feel there is much to be said for looking at other medical traditions too, and somehow blending the best of both worlds. I have read of people who refuse all forms of Western medicine such as chemotherapy, relying solely on traditional Eastern medicine. Some of them survive and thrive, while others ultimately die from their disease. The reverse is also true where many people survive life-threatening cancers relying only on the medical treatments their doctors prescribe, yet there are those too who do not survive. You have to find what you are comfortable with and what works for you. To illustrate how different medical traditions operate, let me bring in Dr David Servan-Schreiber, a medical doctor who survived two bouts of brain cancer but sadly recently passed away. When his oncologist gave him the all-clear after being operated on for the second time, he couldn't really believe that was the end of the story. So he went on his own journey of research and discovery to find out what he could do to prevent the cancer from returning and to understand all the background causes of the disease.

I came across his excellent book *Anti Cancer: A New Way*

of Life several years into my cancer journey and it reinforced, among many other things, some of the ideas I had previously read about concerning the differences between Eastern and Western approaches to medical treatment. Working in a humanitarian mission in Tibet, Dr Servan-Schreiber realised that there were two healthcare systems in operation: a modern, Western hospital and a medical school that taught traditional Tibetan medicine, which was based on strengthening the body to tackle the disease rather than addressing the symptoms. Practices such as meditation, herbal infusions and diet modifications were the core of their treatments. He questioned many of the doctors there: when faced with a dilemma, do you choose Western medicine or your own ancient medicine? They looked at him strangely. 'But it's obvious … if it is an acute illness like pneumonia, an infarction, or appendicitis, you have to see Western doctors. They have fast, efficient treatments for crises and accidents. But if it's a chronic disease, then you should see a Tibetan doctor. The treatments take longer but they treat the terrain in depth. In the long term it's the only thing that really works.'

Today, 90% of medical conditions are classified as chronic, slow-developing diseases, caused by inflammation in the body as a result of our lifestyles, and although medical advances have meant that the symptoms can often be controlled, many of these are not totally cured by drugs or surgery. Cancer is now being thought of as a chronic disease, where it can take anywhere between one and forty years for a cancer cell to become a dangerous tumour. As Dr Servan-Schreiber discovered in Tibet, modern Western medicine is usually needed to deal with the acute phase of the illness, but to prevent cancer occurring in the first place and for those that want to remain in remission once treated, it is often Eastern traditional medical methods that are more successful.

The focus of much of Western medicine is still on illness as opposed to wellness, treating symptoms of disease rather than focusing on its prevention. With an explosion in the number of people with chronic nonlife-threatening diseases, surely a different approach needs to be taken, in order to make these people 'well'. In the scientific post-industrial revolution of the Western world, the ancient wisdom of healing that focuses on the soul and mind, and not just the repair of the physical body, has somehow gotten lost.

Showing vulnerability

Such a holistic focus often requires a person to open up their heart to new ideas, and this is not something that everyone is capable of or wishes to do, because it takes courage and means you have to overcome fear and admit vulnerability. By doing so, you are allowing yourself to be raw and vulnerable, admitting to others that you are scared and need help. With our lifestyles today, we have in some way lost touch with our deeper selves and the connection between the mind and body. It is no wonder that chronic illnesses, so often attributable to our stressful lifestyles, are on the increase. We have become the masters of subversion and submission, not allowing our authentic selves to manifest, and when our expectations are not met, stress builds up in our minds and bodies. At least the subject of mental health is now being discussed far more openly than in the past, and the stigma associated with it is far less than in previous generations. The current pandemic has created even more stress in the lives of millions of people and there is no doubt that in the coming years, mental health issues will continue to rise.

In times gone by, illness was often not discussed within a family, especially not with young children. I remember as a child we never knew when someone was ill, or in some cases even passed away. I was twenty-four when my grandmother died; it wasn't until many years after her death that I found out that she had breast cancer. In my parents' circle, cancer was a disease which was referred to in Yiddish as *yenna makka* (that plague), and since my Yiddish at that time wasn't quite up to scratch, we never knew what they were talking about. Yet even today there are many people who, when diagnosed with a serious illness, be it cancer or anything else, prefer to stay quiet and not talk about it in the community. This decision has to be acknowledged and accepted as that family's way of dealing with it. That was how Johnny and I dealt with it when I was first diagnosed. We only shared the news with our immediate family. But once I started treatment, our children, who lived in Israel and were not available to offer ongoing help, pleaded with us to share with family friends so we could receive additional support. It was at that point that I did confide in a few close family members and friends. Eventually, several months later, when I could not attend my niece's wedding as I had started treatment, my cancer became public knowledge.

I believe that previous generations were afraid to show any vulnerability, lest it be perceived as a weakness. So many of that age group had gone through a war, where they had to be strong to survive in the face of so much death and destruction. Perhaps that was why so much was hidden away and left unsaid. It was their protective mechanism.

Today in the new environment of a Corona world, we are all living with a degree of vulnerability, which comes not just from the uncertainty of the whole situation and the inability to plan anything, but also from the worry, anxiety and stress that affect us mentally and physically. If we can acknowledge our vulnerability, we should be able to develop an attitude where we take responsibility, which is 'response-ability', the ability to respond to it. And during this pandemic, we have seen many people responding in positive ways: from neighbourhood support groups to the setting up of virtual platforms for connecting across the world for business, education, culture and numerous other areas of communal life.

There is an interesting parallel here regarding vulnerability and cancer. Undergoing any form of chemotherapy is likely to create a physical vulnerability in the body as it suppresses the immune system, killing some healthy cells along with the diseased ones. Furthermore, when you sign the consent forms for treatment, they clearly state a possible side effect of the treatment is the emergence of other cancers in the body. Going through a stem cell transplant, or indeed any type of transplant, is the ultimate state of physical vulnerability, as your entire immune system has to be eradicated beforehand in order for your body to accept the new cells or organs. And in the months following a transplant you are put on immunosuppressant drugs so that your body will not reject these new cells or organs. The stem cell transplant itself was one of the most difficult times for me and my family, when I was vulnerable both physically and mentally. I tried to stay positive, in an attempt to find wellness in the midst of my illness, but it wasn't easy.

In a way, what I went through with my transplant, where I physically opened up my body to vulnerability to ensure its transformation for healing, was what I had internalised and practised from a psychological and holistic perspective. The physical external state was an opening for an analogous experience in the inner metaphysical realm.

During my illness I had recognised my vulnerability; going public was an acknowledgement of my condition and an admission that I needed support. And this was scary in the beginning. But I feel deeply that the incredible support I received from my family, friends and community helped me to heal. The love and positive vibes I received by opening my heart to all those around me allowed the energy to flow from them to me, and this helped to create positivity inside me, allowing me to heal. I also attribute this positivity to my mother's strong genes. She was the most 'glass half full' person you could ever hope to meet.

Power of the mind

Today there is scientific evidence for the existence of energy fields that connect all beings through emotions, especially love. The positive flow of energy that this connection creates can really have a measurable healing effect. I feel sure that this is what happened with me as it has been known for many years that generally people who have a more positive outlook on life cope better in almost any situation, be it ill health, bereavement, relationships or money problems.

Forty years ago, Dr Bernie Siegel, an American physician, wrote a series of books describing how the mind can influence the body and help it to heal. He focused on patients suffering from a range of diseases who had defied the statistical odds against them. He felt that if they had nothing in common then he could put it down to errors in diagnosis, luck or spontaneous remissions. In his book *Peace, Love and Healing*, Dr Siegel observed that these people did share something. 'They all are manifesting the same basic qualities; peace of mind, the capacity for unconditional love, the courage to be themselves, a feeling of control over their lives, independence, an acceptance of responsibility for decisions affecting their lives and the ability to express their feelings.'

These were patients who were finding wellness within illness. Their illness had put them on a path to self-realisation. Their healing was coming from remembering who they were, and perhaps that is one of the deepest lessons I learnt through my experience with cancer and the very difficult treatments I had to endure. Dr Siegel observed how the physiological effects of love, hope and a positive state of mind helped many of his patients achieve remission and cures from a range of illnesses. Although his observations had not been backed up by detailed medical research, many of the results were undeniable.

One of Dr Siegel's books found its way into my life in the early years of my cancer journey. *How To Be an Exceptional Patient* explores many of the factors which led to the recovery of some of his patients: the importance of the doctors and patient's family sharing in the mindset of hope; the power of the subconscious mind; and the patient actively participating in their own treatment. It shone a light for me as I stared down the deep, dark tunnel that a cancer journey can sometimes be and gave me hope that maybe I too could become an 'exceptional patient'. Reading Sophie Sabbage's book helped me explore many of his ideas at a much deeper and more practical level, and all of this added to my growing knowledge of how I could navigate my way through my cancer journey.

In recent years there have been many more scientific studies to try to explain exactly why and how the mind can control and

16

create physical changes in the body. The whole new science of epigenetics and the increasing scientific research into understanding the mind-body connection have led to an interest in more spiritual and natural approaches to healing, many of which I will discuss in subsequent pathways.

But one of the important things to acknowledge is that when you are in the midst of a difficult challenge, is it not easy to be positive. In fact trying to continually stay positive can have a negative impact on your health as feelings of guilt can arise when you aren't able to assuage the pain you are going through. I experienced my fair share of frustration when trying to be positive.

It's a choice

DIARY ENTRY: *June 2016*

I actually have had enough. Enough of doctors, nurses and hospitals, enough of cannulas and pic lines, enough of injections, tablets, nausea, extreme tiredness, fuzzyheaded, waiting rooms and waiting hours. It comes to a point where it just gets too much of too many things in too big a dose in too protracted a period of time, and it is all-encompassing and overwhelming. However, with all of this I try to remind myself that I am one of the lucky ones. I thank God every day that at least I have not had to put up with enduring pain. Then things could really become unbearable.

Even an optimistic, positive person, which I try very hard to be, can have their off days. Those closest to me understand this, especially Johnny and he gives me space, but always tries to make me see something positive or try and rest until I feel better. And inevitably I do because there is so much to be grateful for. The expertise of the doctors, the kind, efficient nurses, the incredibly equipped hospitals, the easy methods of delivering the most up-to-date medicines, the ability to control side effects, the pleasant waiting rooms... The list is endless.

So it's all a matter of perspective and one is allowed to view things from both sides. Rarely do I allow myself any self-pity, but occasionally I feel like I could scream from the rooftops: 'It's not fair…why me?' I've been through my fair share of medical procedures, emergencies and treatments in the past few years and if there's one thing I have learnt it is that there is always, but always, someone in a worse position than you. And not just someone, but thousands of people. So I count my blessings daily and go forward in the best way I can…Because I know the answer to 'why me?' is 'why not me?'

Asking yourself 'why me?' turns you into a victim. If you change the question to 'why not me?', you change the paradigm and you become a survivor. You are a person who has overcome, and will continue to overcome, the challenges in your life. It is all a matter of perception and determination.

Since writing this entry over four years ago, I have come to realise that going through an illness or any challenge in life begs the question 'why me?', which is not always answerable by changing the focus to 'why not me?'. In many ways, it reflects the universal question of why do bad things happen to good people, and this touches on issues regarding our faith and religious values. What is important to realise is that a challenge – whether an illness or otherwise – is not a punishment, but rather a wakeup call, a call-to-action and an invitation to awaken you to your true purpose. Challenges open the door to finding that deep wellspring of healing that can guide you on your path. A crisis allows you to go deep inside yourself, and find that inner voice that will help you transform a negative attitude into something more positive, and I believe this is what helped me as I took a more holistic approach to my illness.

One fundamental problem is the way illness and death are perceived as enemies that have to be fought. The implication is that if you succumb to your illness, you have 'lost the battle' and somehow didn't fight hard enough. This is simply *not* true in most cases. Everyone dies at some point from something, and having a judgemental attitude (even if it is intended to be encouraging or motivating) creates stress for the patients and their families, building an atmosphere of fear, when what they really need is love and support and an understanding of what they are going through.

Finding wellness is also about making choices, and believe me, there were so many choices I had to make during my cancer journey. I have lost count of the intense meetings, phone calls and emails we had with my medical teams, firstly at the Royal Marsden Hospital and later University College London Hospital (UCLH). Difficult decisions had to be made as my illness transformed from an indolent low-grade lymphoma to a much more aggressive, high-grade dangerous one.

Years back, when I first went to my doctor feeling unwell, and he realised that there was something wrong with my blood tests results, he referred me to a haematology consultant, who was not the most endearing character. But we were so overwhelmed by my cancer diagnosis that even Johnny, who ordinarily was a good judge of character, didn't see that this doctor wasn't the right person to take my cancer journey forward. It was only several months later when Ian, my son-in-law who is a colorectal surgeon, came to an appointment with me and spoke to my consultant that we all realised something wasn't adding up. Haematology is not Ian's area of speciality, but he has a doctor's intuition and it was then that we decided to go for a second opinion. And this is where we struck gold.

I had done some research into the best doctors in London for CLL and found a haemato-oncology specialist at the Royal Marsden Hospital called Dr Claire Dearden. After meeting her for the first time, we realised we had found the right person to hold our hands and guide us through the next part of the journey. She was the most compassionate, reassuring, but also pragmatic specialist one could hope for, and her upbeat attitude towards my illness and treatment definitely helped me stay positive. She took me through the early years of my treatment, greeted me with a smile at every appointment and maintained a can-do attitude to whatever roadblock arose. Her enduring message was that as long as we had another option to try if one treatment wasn't working, there was always hope.

But when I had to undergo a stem cell transplant, due to practical logistics and insurance, I had to leave Dr Dearden's care and move to UCLH. Fortunately, the Bone Marrow Transplant (BMT) unit at UCLH is also one of the most highly regarded in the country. And the team there gave me the same amazing care as I received at the Marsden. From the consultants to the doctors and nurses, from the catering staff to the medical auxiliaries and cleaning staff, they were the most professional, kind and caring group of people. I was truly blessed to be surrounded by such an incredible team as I not only had to contend with a very complicated medical procedure, but also ended up staying in hospital for three months. I am convinced that being surrounded by the right people helps you to heal.

At that time, I decided to add a private haematologist to my medical team who was also one of the top oncology doctors in the field. He was our second opinion guy, whose advice and reassurance played a big part in many of the decisions we made about my treatment. As with Dr Dearden, from our first meeting with Professor John Gribben, Johnny and I knew we had found another pair of invaluable hands to hold ours through the difficult journey ahead. I did not tell anyone else on my medical team at the time that we were seeing Professor Gribben because he wasn't treating me; his role was more to review with us all the suggestions my doctors had made so we would be clear about all the options available when it came to having to make decisions. It turned out that he was the one who not only initially suggested investigating a new treatment option in the States called CAR-T therapy, but also provided us with the contacts at hospitals there. He knew of these hospitals' successes with the new treatments not yet available in the UK, as he had sent some of his patients to them. My medical teams in UCLH, who were all excellent, worked with me on this too. But it was his final push to 'get on a plane now' when the second top-up from my stem cell transplant failed, that gave us the impetus to fly to Florida for the CAR-T cell treatment.

It was there that Dr Fred Locke and his team at the Moffitt Cancer Centre in Tampa took over. Like so many of my doctors in London, Dr Locke is not only a top professional in his field, but he has a humble, caring and wise nature that belies his young age. Together with the incredible staff and facilities in hospital, my hand was held every step of the way through my two months of treatment there. In this specialist cancer centre, they take a much more holistic approach to healing than in many of the centres in the UK. I was completely blown away by what was on offer for the patients in terms of complimentary therapy, which aids recovery. Apart from the art therapists who would arrive in my room complete with a full complement of materials with which to paint and even create origami figures, I had access to a harpist who would play for me, a massage therapist and a reflexologist. I know that in some specialist cancer centres in the UK, such services are available, but not usually for inpatients undergoing treatment within the actual hospitals themselves. So yes, it was a very different type of experience. I am not going to go into the differences between private medical treatment in America and the NHS in the UK. Suffice to say that all NHS services are provided free at the point of delivery, something unheard of in America, and I owe my life to the incredible staff that work tirelessly in it.

It was a friend who worked in medical research who connected me with Professor Gribben, and it was through him and Dr Claire Roddie, my CAR-T team specialist at UCLH, that we eventually reached Dr Locke. That is why it is important to reach out to others in the know, who can help with ideas and finding the right contacts. Finding wellness in illness is, as I said, also about finding the right people to help you.

Years before I was diagnosed with cancer, I had to have a hip replacement operation and one of the people who entered my life at the time to help with my rehabilitation was Cruella, my personal trainer. This incredibly fit, quirky and caring woman has become a permanent fixture in my life, because not only is she an excellent trainer, she also knows exactly where I am at, in terms of my physical mobility and stamina, before each session starts. She can tell from the minute she walks into the room if I am holding myself at an angle or if I'm feeling a bit 'off' that day, and she tailors the session to my needs. This intuitiveness was invaluable when I was going through my years of chemotherapy. She would sit me in a chair and work to keep me mobile with my limited strength.

The same has been true for many of the therapists and counsellors I worked with at Chai, the Jewish Cancer charity, where I enjoyed many different types of sessions – from massage, reiki and cranial osteopathy to diet advice and counselling on my state of mind. Often, I would have several sessions in one type of therapy, find that they were no longer as effective, and move on to another type of therapy. It goes back to what I discussed about being open to suggestions in trying to find what works for you.

My wonderfully calm and compassionate yoga teacher Barbara, who for over twenty years put up with my weekly kvetching as I tried to get into the appropriate poses, was another angel in my repertoire of support that has kept me going. She introduced me to the benefits of meditation, which admittedly I didn't fully appreciate before my illness, and she became a treasured friend who has helped guide me in other areas of my life. She recently retired but we still keep in touch, and I was lucky to find Julia to take her place; these days, attending Julia's over-sixties yoga class keeps me agile, calm and relaxed.

Everyone has to make choices on myriads of different issues throughout their lives. However, when you are ill and have choices about various medical treatments, which will hopefully cure you, but might come with serious side effects that could also kill you, those choices become very difficult. How do you decide? How do you try to navigate your way through the minefield that is the world of medical treatments? Although in my case I was dealing specifically with cancer, this is equally true for all types of illnesses. What can guide you through this journey?

In my quest to heal, I didn't just have to consider which approach worked best for me but also had to choose the best people to work with. Whether it is the doctors and hospitals, or the therapists and lifestyle advisors, each person is going to have an impact on your journey from illness to wellness, so you need to choose well. You need to be aware of exactly how they are assisting you, if you feel they understand you and if they are helping you move in the right direction. This is not always easy, and you have to develop a sense of your own wellbeing to judge what is right for you.

Once you have a diagnosis and a plan of action from your doctors, the next link in the chain of decision-making is your family, especially if the treatment involves possibly serious side effects. At each stage in my cancer treatment journey, I discussed the scenarios with my family, looking at all the pros and cons, but in the end, they always said it was my decision. The most critical decision of all for us came in September 2016: whether or not to go ahead with a stem cell transplant which offered a 50/50 chance of a total cure but a 20% possibility that I could die either from the transplant itself or from complications afterwards. One of the key points that Dr Dearden, my doctor at the time, told us was that it was important that the whole family make a unified decision, since she had seen families torn apart by differences in opinion when things had gone badly wrong. I was blessed that my family were united not just in this, but in so many other decisions we had made. It was the best chance I had for a possible cure and they knew I wanted to take that chance. So how did I finally decide?

This is where your internal guidance system comes in to play – a subject I devote an entire pathway to: listening to the wisdom of your heart. In many instances it is referred to as a gut feeling and scientific studies have shown that the gut does indeed control so many aspects of our health. Yet the newest science now points to the heart being the 'mind' of the body, not the brain, and it is through an understanding of heart wisdom that you can make the choices that are right for you. Trying to decide on so many aspects of treatment is not easy, but once you are focused on finding that wellness inside your illness, once you realise that your illness is a wakeup call, the choices you make become clearer.

But perhaps the biggest choice you need to make is the attitude with which you choose to go forward as this will affect every aspect of your healing. Attitude is everything, for it will dictate the paths you take and if you truly want to find wellness within illness, you will.

Stepping  Stones

Lessons I have learnt about finding wellness within illness

- There is no one right way to heal.
- Disease in the body really means that the body is suffering from 'dis-ease'. It is not at ease or at peace with itself.
- Your physical wellbeing is deeply connected to your mental, emotional and spiritual wellbeing.
- Healing does not necessarily imply the 'curing' of illness.
- Think and look outside the box to gather information from different sources and adapt it to suit what will work for you.
- Alternative therapies to conventional medicine may provide extra support and alleviate symptoms but always inform your medical team about any other therapies you are considering.
- Acknowledge your vulnerability but do not let it overwhelm you.
- Try to create a good support team around you with people you trust and can work with, both medically and personally.

- Keep notes on all your medical tests and letters and prepare questions to discuss with your medical team at the next consultation. Be open to suggestions but make your own decisions, based on the best information you have at the time.

- Taking back control over your life in any small way during illness can help promote a better emotional framework.

Pathway Two

Coping with Loss –
Learning to Grieve

'Healing from loss does not mean the loss didn't happen, it means it no longer controls us.'

— DAVID KESSLER

DIARY ENTRY: *April 2018*

I was listening to the radio last week when a guest on Radio 4's Desert Island Discs was talking about watching her children dancing at a family celebration and she turned to her husband, saying to him, 'Grab my hand and savour the moment...'

That one line she uttered towards the end of the programme cut through me like a knife, shaking me to the very core. The intensity of that moment's realisation, that never ever again will I be able to grab Johnny's hand and savour the moment. Never again would there be that intimate space between us as we delighted in a shared moment of joy. The finality of his death came crashing down again, as it had done at disparate moments over the past four months. Thankfully during most of these moments I have been alone and able to let the tears flow without burdening any of my family and friends with the grief that occasionally engulfed me. But after the grief lessened, I had to remind myself that we did share so many precious moments in our forty years together.

Stopping to smell the roses, making hay while the sun shines, ensuring that times together were enjoyed to the full with and without the wider family...but can you ever have enough of those? Can one's soul be satiated when it is fully aware that the years stretch ahead with unfulfilled promise; with family celebrations yet to come, with untold stories of escapades not yet undertaken?

Memories are wonderful and I am immensely blessed to have so many good ones of Johnny and our family over the years. But memory is a bank of deposits where the interest gets paid out over the years. Who will put in the new deposits to accrue the capital that will pay out such rich dividends in the future? I comfort myself with the thought that my children and my wider family all deeply cherish Johnny's memory and know that his gift for telling a good story will pass on to the next generation with pride.

So no, I can no longer savour the moment with Johnny, but hopefully there will be many more moments to celebrate and share and more memories to create with all the family in years to come.

In the past thirty years I have suffered the loss of many older family members, including my parents, my in-laws and several dear close friends, but nothing could have prepared me for the sudden and untimely death of my husband, Johnny. The visceral experience of him being so cruelly and unexpectedly cut out of my life caused my world to come crashing down. I was not even in the same country as him when it happened; I was not at his bedside as he took his last breath. And this has haunted me ever since, but I try to see this as God's grace in that I did not have to witness my most beloved's life slip away in front of my eyes.

We were in Israel on holiday visiting our children when Johnny contracted pneumonia. Once hospitalised, they discovered that he had other health issues that were affecting his recovery. I had to return to London for urgent medical tests following my stem cell transplant and was reassured by the doctors and my children that all Johnny needed was a few weeks to fully recover and then he would be able to travel home with one of the children accompanying him. So the last time I was physically with Johnny was in hospital two days before he died. I spoke to him on FaceTime the day he died and things looked like they were improving – he even managed to question our son Baruch about what was happening in the business. But later that evening, out of the blue he started coughing up blood and went into heart failure.

I will never forget the look on my sister Dina's face as she arrived at our house to break the news to Baruch and me. My son Avi had called her from Israel to come round and tell us. His brother Natan had been with Johnny in the hospital when he died and was in deep shock, unable to talk to me directly. Hearing Dina say the words that Johnny had died was surreal in that it didn't feel like reality, yet I knew it was real. I knew it had happened and I knew that as my world was collapsing around me, the last thing I could afford to do was collapse. In so many cases the first reaction to hearing tragic news is denial, where you feel a burning sense of 'this cannot be true'. Yet that didn't happen with me. I accepted the fact that Johnny was dead. I accepted it because I knew there was nothing I could do at that moment that would bring him back, and there was much to organise in order for us to get to Israel for the funeral and the *shivah*.[1]

That fateful night when we heard the news, one of the first people to arrive at our home was the rabbi of our synagogue, Rabbi Mordechai Ginsbury. And like so many of the special people who have helped me along my journey, he and his wife Judy have been absolute rocks of support for my family throughout the difficult

---

1. A period of seven days of formal mourning for the dead, beginning immediately after the funeral.

years. Our connection with him has been more a personal friendship than him just being our spiritual advisor, and he was totally
distraught at hearing of Johnny's sudden death. As more and
more of our family and friends gathered in our home that evening
to share the burden of grief with me, I remember thinking with
a deep-seated belief: 'We will get through this. We are a strong
family and I come from a long line of strong women and we will
get through this together.' I believe that the internal resolve and
strength I somehow garnered from deep inside me came partly
from the years I had spent dealing with my cancer, but was also
partly inherited from my parents' strong genes of having survived
hardships in their lives, and witnessing how my mother had coped
with my father's sudden death.

Somehow, I switched into practical mode, which has always
been my forte. I closed down my emotions during those crucial
hours in order to get done what needed to be done. I knew if I let
go for one minute the floodgates would open and they would be
impossible to shut. Each time the doorbell rang that night, and
another friend or family member came round to console us, I
braced myself for the inevitable flow of emotion and forced myself
to greet them as best I could. I don't know how I managed to get
through the next thirty-six hours until we arrived at the cemetery
in Israel where I finally witnessed Johnny's lifeless body being
lowered into his grave. It was then that the floodgates burst open
and I collapsed in grief as his death and loss became actualised.

How does one heal after loss? How does one move from a life
you had all planned out to one that can no longer fulfil its promises?
Grief is the way. You need to grieve and internalise that the people
and things you once had, or the activities you were once able to
do, are no longer. It is moving from the life you expected to the life
you are now faced with. It is exchanging a life that was once normal
for one that is anything but normal. It is the pain you suffer as you
grieve over your dreams of what should have been. You need to
acknowledge your grief, to open yourself up to what you are going

through, so that your heart can be open to a greater capacity and as you break open the wounds, you can start to heal.

This important lesson is reflected in Rachel Naomi Remen's book *My Grandfather's Blessings*, where she writes: 'Every great loss demands that we choose life again. We need to grieve in order to do this. The pain we have not grieved over will always stand between us and life. When we don't grieve a part of you becomes stuck in the past...'

Grief comes in many guises and is experienced in many different ways. If you experience true love in its many manifestations, whether for a parent, a sibling, a child, a close friend or a spouse who is your life partner in every way, you have invested in a relationship which can make you vulnerable. It can bring with it pain, but you have to be open to that possibility in order to have a meaningful relationship. So when that love is lost through separation or death, grief is the consequence. Why does grief hurt so much? Because you are experiencing the profound loss of losing something that has become part of you.

I came across the author Jeff Foster through my yoga teacher Julia, and I found that so much of what he, a survivor of serious depression, writes about the 'wordless essence of life', resonated deeply with me regarding the challenges in my life. In his book *Falling in Love with Where You Are*, he writes about why grief hurts so much: '[It is because] you've actually lost a part of yourself, a part of you that made you feel fully yourself, and that's why it hurts so much... How can son be son without a father? How can wife be wife without a husband?'

If you love someone you will at some time grieve; love and grief are the two sides of the same coin.

Stages of grief

Like so many things in life, grief is a necessary process that one has to live through and experience in order to come out the other side. Denial, anger, bargaining, depression and acceptance are all stages one goes through during the grief process and are a well-documented phenomenon known as the Kübler-Ross Grief Cycle. Although these stages do not necessarily occur in a specific order, most of them will be experienced at some point in the months and years following a loss, and it is important to realise that they are descriptive rather than prescriptive. Grief has come to me in many waves in diverse arenas as I confronted my different challenges over the years, and I have passed through all these stages, though not in a linear fashion. It has been more as an ebb and flow between varying emotions at different times.

Acceptance is normally recognised as the last stage of the grief cycle, but for me, when I heard that Johnny had died, it was the first. In many ways this defence mechanism reflected how I had dealt with my cancer over the years. Each time I had chemotherapy or tests I tried to move on the minute they were over by externalising the experience, by moving it to the back of my consciousness. Each person finds their own way to cope with challenges and this was my way of coping at the time with my cancer; the treatment happened, it's over, now on to the next thing. I put the experience out of my mind, but what I realised later was that this coping mechanism which worked for me then meant that I had not internalised what had happened. And perhaps this was true with Johnny's death. At that time, I didn't realise that by failing to internalise the experience, I could not fully heal myself. Despite having some of the tools needed to deal with grief, due to having coped with my cancer diagnosis six years earlier, I don't think I allowed it to penetrate inwards to my soul in the year following his death. Not allowing myself to fully deal with Johnny's death was, I recognised, a coping strategy that I needed to adopt in order for me to retain my energy to deal with my ongoing cancer treatment. My daughter tried to persuade me to have some bereavement counselling, but I told her I was not yet ready for it, because I needed to have the energy to physically and mentally heal myself from my cancer before I could deal with the emotional turmoil that I suspected would result from opening myself up to discussing my feelings about Johnny's death.

You might think that in accepting Johnny's death from the beginning I refused to deny it and refused to be angry at the situation. But you would be wrong. There were many moments in the months that followed when I did get angry. I was angry with God, and angry with everyone and everything. But I let it flow through me; I knew I had to experience that anger so I could move forward.

When my father died so many years ago, I was not able to deal with his loss adequately, with the grief his passing caused. I had young children, life was extremely hectic, and I wasn't in the frame of mind to seek any sort of bereavement counselling. There is no doubt that his death left me with unresolved issues, but I didn't give myself time to reflect on what his passing meant to me. I think part of my reaction was influenced by my mother's attitude; she was not one to sit around moping. Instead, she got on with all the practicalities that needed to be dealt with. In fact, I don't think in the year following his death I ever saw my mother once cry or break down. She was stoic but not unemotional, and although we knew she missed our father deeply, she never wore her grief on her sleeve. She did her mourning in private. She loved us deeply and carried on his role as the head of the family, something she continued to do for another twenty-six years until her passing at age ninety-one.

She had a wonderful way of looking at life. I will never forget at my niece's wedding some years after my father died, I looked at her basking in the joy of such a happy occasion and asked her, 'Don't you miss Daddy at these moments? It's so sad that he is not here to share it with us.' Such was her attitude that she smiled at me and said, 'Yes it is, and I do miss him, but I am so lucky as I have a double portion of *nachas*[2]: his *and* mine.' The grief was there but I don't think she had internalised it, as she didn't dwell on it. It was only after Johnny died that we felt the grief she had bottled up for all those years finally come out. Her mental health took a very steep decline from then on, as she began to disengage

---

2. Joy and pride.

from her surroundings. She could not reconcile Johnny's death, her Johnny, who was a son to her, with her deep faith in God who looks after all the family. We felt that Johnny's death rekindled in her the emotions of grief from my father's death that she had tried so hard to bury years earlier. I honestly believe that she was doubly affected by his death because she had not fully processed her grief for her husband at the time.

It was heartbreaking to see my mother suffer after Johnny's death, to know that she was looking at me, her daughter, who had lost her husband while away on holiday, after recently celebrating our fortieth wedding anniversary, just as she and my father had done before his untimely death. Still, she carried on, although I could feel that the grief she suffered caused the light to go out from her eyes.

Almost eight months after Johnny died, my mother passed away, peacefully in her own home. I wasn't there at the time, just as I wasn't at Johnny's bedside when he passed away. I feel that God in His ultimate mercy had spared me the trauma of seeing two of my most beloveds take their last breaths. For being present when a loved one dies is surely one of life's most harrowing experiences.

Although I was bereft, the grief I experienced at my mother's death was different to that of Johnny's. She had lived a very full life and had experienced enormous *nachas* from her many grandchildren and greatgrandchildren. Her *shivah* was more a celebration of her incredible life, from a Kindertransport refugee arriving on these shores at the age of eleven, unable to speak a word of English, to the matriarch of a large, growing and successful family that spanned four generations living in the UK and Israel. I was happy she was finally at peace, no longer suffering. The memories that the family shared during the week of *shivah* were priceless, especially as we sat *shivah* in her home, the house she had lived in for over fifty-five years, the home we had all grown up in. It was full of happy childhood memories, ours and those of our children. All of this helped assuage the grief her passing left in a way that was different to what I had to deal with when Johnny died.

Since Johnny's death, grief has overwhelmed me at various unexpected moments and in different levels of anguish. The deep-seated grief that caused tears to flow freely down my face and my body to shake did not last long, thankfully. I let the emotion engulf me, to fully feel the pain of Johnny's loss. I needed it; I needed to wallow in the sorrow of my loss that had created such a deep vacuum. It was then that I felt his absence so acutely. But there were moments when the grief was lighter, when someone would do or say something that reminded me of Johnny, which revived positive memories. It was then I felt his presence. I held the memories of how things had been.

DIARY ENTRY: *June 2018*

'We know not the place where our loved ones are – we know the place where they are not.'

These lines resonated deeply within me, as I came across them written about a funeral in the wonderful book I am currently reading, The House by the Lake. It is this thought, of the sheer unknowability of the afterlife that begs the question: Where does the man with whom I have spent the past forty years currently reside?

'In shamayim,'[3] my grandchildren tell me. 'Don't worry Savti,[4] Sabba[5] is in shamayim and Hashem[6] is looking after him.' The simplicity of children's thinking is sometimes easier to accept than the complexity of a reality that we do not know or understand.

Every Friday night as I light my candles to usher in Shabbat, I pray for Hashem to look after Johnny and for Johnny to look after all of us. But I often wonder, 'Where are you, Johnny?'

---

3. Heaven.
4. Grandma.
5. Grandpa.
6. God.

During the shivah I told my family and friends who were close to Johnny that each person carried a bit of Johnny's neshamah[7] inside their own neshamot. When my two eldest grandchildren went to visit Johnny's matzevah,[8] I told them that it is only his body that is there; his neshamah and spirit and the fullness of life that exuded from him is now within all of us.

'…We know the place where they are not.' Johnny is not here. He will not be walking through the door, regaling us with another of his great stories, lighting up the room with his smile and warm personality. He is not here physically, but I feel his presence and essence at different times and in different places. As the days go by, there is occasionally some incident that will trigger a deep emotion in me and an awareness that Johnny's neshamah is connecting to mine.

At an outdoor concert I recently went to, as my first outing since finishing treatment, Katherine Jenkins sang 'Time to say goodbye,' a song made famous by Andrea Bocelli, and Johnny's favourite song. It left me in floods of tears, as I felt Johnny was right there sitting with me. At times like this I tend to look upwards towards the heavens and in that deep blue sky I find a sense of solace. It was that same solace that I found when I spent time in Netanya after the shivah. Looking at the sea and the vast sky with its incredible sunsets, I felt Johnny's presence deeply.

Am I at peace? I have periods of acceptance, yet also periods of anger. I have moments of melancholy and grief, yet also manage to have times of laughter and happiness too. I know Johnny is no longer here, but where he is now I can only surmise. I just pray that he is at peace and watching over us all.

---

7. Soul.
8. Gravestone.

Many shades of grief

Although the death of a loved one tends to be the rawest and deepest level of grief, you can also grieve the loss of something you hold dear: the loss of a future you envisaged, the loss of your health, the loss of your career, the loss of your marriage or any relationship. Basically, any ideal that has been brutally punctured by reality. Some of the most moving articles I have read about the loss of a former life were written by Melanie Reid, the Times journalist who broke her neck in a riding accident. Living life from a wheelchair completely changed her perspective, yet she writes with humour, irony and almost no self-pity. But occasionally grief seeps into her life, as she mourns her loss of independence.

There was much to grieve following my cancer diagnosis: things that may seem small yet were an integral part of my life. I am an avid swimmer. Many years ago, after a back injury sustained during my gap year working on Kibbutz Lavi, I started seeing an osteopath in London. She recommended swimming as the best exercise to help keep my back in shape. I laughed when she told me this because, despite weekly swimming lessons for two years during secondary school, I could barely manage two lengths of a pool with my very ungainly breaststroke. She told me that I should learn to swim properly, specifically with my head in the water, to avoid any neck strain. Easier said than done. But needs must and my back needed looking after. Within a year of this very timely advice I had learnt to swim up to forty lengths at a time and both my breaststroke and crawl were deftly executed as I surged along the swimming lanes at my local health club.

Swimming became not just my physical therapy but my mental therapy too. I loved my time in the water where at least twice a week I would think through so many things in my head as I swam up and down, toning my body and honing my mind. This became the classic 'me time' that in recent years has become so fashionable an asset in the crazy, busy world we now inhabit. I would often meet my friends at the pool for a coffee and a schmooze afterwards; it was the perfect combination of exercise and socialising.

However, once I was diagnosed with lymphoma, and my treatment began, I could no longer use public swimming pools for risk of infection. And this for me was not just detrimental because I could no longer exercise, it was a mental and emotional loss as well.

If I think about what I miss most since cancer came into my life, regular swimming time would feature high on the list. In a way, I have been grieving over this loss for many years. My body craves that gentle exercise that keeps the joints and muscles in good working order. Somehow regular walking and even the yoga classes that I so enjoy don't give me the same feeling I used to get gliding through water. Now the only time I get to swim is when I go out to Israel where I'm lucky enough to have a pool almost to myself, and where I get the additional pleasure of the sun on my skin as I swim. The times I spend out there in the water are so precious because they allow me to reconnect to the person I used to be.

Reclaiming back a part of yourself that was lost allows you to heal in some way. That is how I have tried to deal with the grief that arose from each new challenge I faced. Whenever I found myself able to return to some former version of myself from before that loss, I would celebrate each incremental step of my progress. Whether it was my hair that started to grow back each time it fell out after my cancer treatment, the condition of my skin that was softer and less wrinkled after constant creaming, or reclaiming my independence as I started to cook for myself again, with each step forward I could feel myself beginning to heal and the grief lessen.

Becoming a grandma was one of the most positive, lifechanging moments for me. It was an affirmation of life continuing into the next generation. All the years of effort bringing up my children melted away as I held my little, one-hour-old granddaughter in my arms. A new love affair was born in that instant and has continued for the past sixteen years as I have watched my eldest grandchild, Meital, grow into the thoughtful, beautiful teenager she is today. And I have had the same feeling as each new grandchild was born. Each time my love and joy just multiplied over and over again. Even though once Avi and Chanie made *Aliyah*[9] all my grandchildren were living in Israel, we still managed to see them very often. But once my treatment for cancer began, being a grandma was no longer a straightforward experience and in many ways, I felt the loss of being a 'hands-on' grandma, which grieved me deeply.

Previously I was there when each new baby was born, helping the family with everything from cooking meals and laundry to walking the baby and looking after the other children while mum slept. However my cancer treatment not only put a stop to the freedom to travel to Israel whenever I wanted to, it also meant that when I was there my family were so concerned about me overdoing things that they wouldn't let me do anything to help in the domestic sphere, other than play with the children and take them on occasional outings. The saddest part was that I missed the birth of two of my grandchildren because both times I was in the middle of treatment. I insisted on Johnny travelling out after the birth of each child, as it was unfair to the children for neither of us to visit and I knew Johnny needed to have a big *nachas* input to counter everything he was going through in London with me.

But the loss of being a 'hands-on' grandma has caused me grief of a different sort. The loss of a deep-seated need to be 'of use' to my children. To help them out in the same way that my mother and mother-in-law were around to look after me when I had my children and be there when I needed them. Granted that the years of us living in different countries had meant that, unlike so many of my friends in London who are busy with their grandchildren on a regular basis, I could never be on call for lastminute help. However, in times of crisis I had flown out to help look after the children. But all of this came to an end with my treatment and it took a long time and many hours of counselling to accept that I had done my job as a mother in bringing up four capable adults who could all now take care of themselves. I had done enough giving in my life

---

9. Immigrated to Israel.

and I should not now feel any guilt or grief about not being able to continue to help them.

And yet, and yet... I did and still do miss that ability to just roll up my sleeves and get on with whatever needs doing each time I visit them. They all shout at me and say, 'You are here; that's enough for us, just enjoy being with the grandchildren and do not think of anything else.' And of course, I do enjoy every single minute with them because I know how precious that time is and who knows when the next visit will be.

Four times during my different cancer treatments, all my hair fell out. For most women this is one of the most difficult side effects of chemotherapy, as their hair so often defines their femininity and who they are. However temporary the loss of hair is, it represents another brick in the wall that has to be climbed to get through treatment; it is another element of the cancer experience to grieve over. For me, my hair loss was not as difficult an issue as it is for other women. This is mainly because for the past forty years as an orthodox Jewish woman I had chosen to cover my hair once I got married. I had never left the house without some form of head covering, be it a hat, scarf or wig. So covering my bald head was really no different to covering my head when it was full of hair. But despite this, I did still feel a sense of grief when faced with the stark reality of my own reflection: the face staring back at me had no hair on its head, no eyebrows and scant few eyelashes. The sense of loss of self, of loss of my personal identity, and facing the reality of my own mortality threatened at times to overwhelm me.

But then, at times when I was completely bald with no makeup on, I would look in the mirror and force myself to say out loud: 'You are beautiful. I love you as you are.' I needed to make these affirmations in order to reassure myself at some of the lowest points during my treatment that I would survive and go on to bigger and better things. I knew then that I would never not love myself for who I am. When I looked in the mirror, I knew that I could also reach inside and touch my authentic self. And that is what I have learnt over these past years. It is what has helped me to heal. I now connect to the self I was born to be, to the self that was neglected throughout the years when I was just too busy 'doing', without time to just be.

There were numerous occasions when I met people during my cancer treatment, and they would express surprise at how well I looked. I always joked with them that I wished my body looked as good inside as it did on the outside. The cancer cells were lurking inside my body, proliferating, and each time I had a scan, I knew that more treatment was on the cards if the cancer had spread. Most people did not see me in my worst state, after days of chemotherapy had completely drained me. By the time I was up and out socialising again, I was in a better state both in my physical appearance and in my mental and emotional mood. Hence the compliments flowed and in a sense distracted me from thinking too deeply about my situation, so I could put the grief over my loss of my hair, my loss of appetite and my deteriorating state of health on the back burner for the time being.

So yes, some losses can be overcome. I tried not to dwell on the things that I have lost because of cancer. I tried to put the losses out of my mind once they passed. This was easier to do when I knew the losses were temporary, like my hair which would inevitably grow back or my swimming which I managed to resume whenever I was in Israel. It was harder to deal with the loss of things that would take much longer to regain – such as having a fully functioning immune system that would allow me to travel freely anywhere anytime; expressing my joy at seeing family and friends by giving them a big hug; having the energy to go out in the evening after a busy day; being able to help my children and grandchildren with whatever chores needed doing. But perhaps my tiredness was not just from treatment and coping with my illness. Talking to friends, I realised we are all ageing and once you are over sixty, you naturally get tired more easily, even if you haven't endured six years of cancer treatment!

But sometimes, you don't just grieve over what you have lost but rather what you never had. This epiphany came to me while watching one of the most emotionally charged films I have ever seen, *Schindler's List*. The film was released several years after my father passed away and brought home in great visual detail some of the horrors my father had experienced during the Holocaust. He had been interred in Plaszow, the work camp that is so brutally portrayed in the film. However hard this was to watch, it was a different scene that caused me tremendous anguish and grief. It was the one in which the Nazis are rounding up a group of Jews to board a train, taking away their suitcases, ostensibly to store in another part of the train. You then see these suitcases being opened and their contents thrown into a pile which is then sorted into different items such as clothes, jewellery, shoes and so on. As the camera pans across these mountains of personal possessions I saw that one of these piles was made up entirely of photographs.

It was then that I felt like a knife had stabbed into the centre of my heart and floods of tears poured from my eyes. Each photograph is a testament to a life lived and to me it represented everything I never knew about my father's family who were murdered by the Nazis, the missing pieces in the puzzle of my family history. We did not possess a single photograph of my father's family or any from his childhood before the war. I had known this as we were growing up, as we used to spend many a Friday night going through all the photographs my parents kept in a huge drawer in our lounge. There were many photographs of every relative imaginable on my mother's side, but not a single one on my father's. I knew he had been through the camps and had lost all his family, but the significance of the lack of family photos did not hit me when I was much younger.

In recent years, I have reflected on the absence of my father's family photographs and wonder if this is why my father was so fascinated with cine film and taking photographs. Whenever there was a family celebration or get-together, or we went on holiday, my father could always be seen with a camera in his hand. In those days, it was either a Kodak or a Canon and you had to send away the film for processing. Several years ago I had all of my father's old 8 mm cine films converted to VHS and it was fascinating to see myself and my family in moving film from when I was four years old, although my children did complain that there was no sound!

My father's keenness to capture precious family moments could have stemmed from a deep psychological need to make sure that these memories were preserved for posterity. He had lost all his family so many years earlier and had no physical reminders of them; he did not want to lose anyone else and needed to keep the memories of his new life alive. And this, I believe, may have helped him to heal, in a way that I described earlier, about regaining some sense of your former self. He did not have his birth family remembered in photos, but he could record his new family. Like so many other aspects of his past, we never discussed this, but when I look back now it seems to make sense to me, as I try to make sense of his life.

Like all emotions, grief falls into a spectrum. The writer Megan Devine watched her partner drown in front of her, three weeks before his fortieth birthday. Even though she was a trained counsellor, this traumatic experience changed the way she approached grief and loss. *It's OK That You Are Not OK* is one of the most practical books I have read about dealing with grief, and although I don't agree with everything she writes, the book does confront the reality of grieving, helping to normalise and validate the experience. Understanding that grief and loss happens to us all at some point in our lives, she discusses the ways in which our culture sees grief as something to be overcome and fixed rather than tended to and supported. She offers ways of helping people through grief and pain by understanding just what it is to live through the reality of loss. She maintains that all grief needs validation but not all grief is the same. Each loss has a different meaning and a different resonance with the sufferer of that loss.

People often say to me: 'You have been through so many challenges. Whatever my challenges in life, they are nowhere as bad as yours.' My response is always that there is no measurement to grief, so you cannot compare one person's challenges and the grief they suffer with another. A shiver went down my spine when I read a similar sentiment in Edith Eger's book *The Choice*. Edith is a remarkable woman who went on to rebuild her life after surviving the horrors of Auschwitz. In her inspiring memoir she recounts her incredible story of resilience and writes '... there is no hierarchy of suffering. There's nothing that makes my pain worse or better than yours... People say to me "Things in my life are pretty hard now, but I have no right to complain – it's not Auschwitz." This kind of comparison can lead us to minimise or diminish our own suffering.'

As I continued to read Edith Eger's book there were further sentiments that caused a bell to chime in my head with regards to my identity as a survivor, especially this: 'Being a survivor, being a "thriver", requires absolute acceptance of what was and what is. If we discount our pain or punish ourselves for feeling lost or isolated or scared about the challenges in our lives, however insignificant these challenges may seem to someone else, then we're still choosing to be victims. We're not seeing our choices. We're judging ourselves.' When I read that page, I had a lightbulb moment as to one of the reasons I decided to write this book, for she finishes the paragraph with these words: 'I don't want you to hear my story and say, "My own suffering is less significant." I want you to hear my story and say "If she can do it then so can I."'

And that is exactly how I feel after reading so many stories of survival and resilience; they have all taught me so much about grief and coping with loss, illness and so many other challenges.

No one has a monopoly on grief. Every person's challenges are different, from bereavement, health or work to money worries or relationship issues. We each need to deal with loss and the grief that resides in our souls. During the Corona pandemic, when everyone has been affected in some way, people have gained an understanding of grief and the part it plays in our lives, from the physical loss of life to the loss of routine and ability to plan ahead. Humanity at large is going through a process of grief and hence we all need to go through processing this grief in order to heal.

Sixth stage of grief: finding meaning

One of the most tragic losses a person can endure is the death of a child. It is heart-wrenching, soul-destroying, and is the deepest wellspring of grief that anyone can imagine. I thank God that I have not experienced it, but I have witnessed it firsthand when some of my friends lost their children. In many ways it is grief at its rawest. One of the most tragic stories I have read about losing children was also one of the most inspiring. In the book *Miriam's Song*, Miriam Peretz tells the story of the death of her two sons in Israel's wars and her husband who died of a broken heart. Grief beyond grief. Unimaginable pain and suffering that could cause the strongest and most courageous person to crumble. Yet her story of strength and resilience, choosing to live a life of hope and bringing inspiration to others, shows how suffering and grief can be turned into something positive, despite the personal toll it takes.

After reading her book, I felt deeply that I needed to make some sort of sense out of Johnny's death. I needed to create a framework in which I could find some kind of meaning, although in reality nothing made sense. One day, while reading book reviews in *The Times* (one of my favourite hobbies), I came across a book by David Kessler called *Finding Meaning: The Sixth Stage of Grief*. He is one of the world's foremost experts on grief and a protégé of Elisabeth Kübler-Ross, the woman who fifty years ago identified the five stages of grief described earlier. I immediately ordered it and, upon reading it, I discovered some very important thoughts and lessons about coping with bereavement. In this book, Kessler discusses a sixth stage to the grief process which he describes as finding meaning. He writes that once the person experiencing the loss can reach a state of acceptance, then a transformation can occur through finding some kind of meaning in that loss. He maintains that 'Loss can wound and paralyse. It can hang over us for years. But finding meaning in loss empowers us to find a path forward. Meaning helps us make sense of grief.'

David Kessler works with many bereaved people, but when his own son tragically died, he was completely overcome and wasn't sure he would be able to live again, never mind work again. 'I had been in such deep pain that I didn't know if meaning was possible after such a shattering loss. But it turned out that in exploring the search for meaning in the devastation of loss, I have discovered that meaning is both possible and necessary.'

But what does meaning look like? Kessler maintains that 'It can take many shapes, such as finding gratitude for the time they had with loved ones, or finding ways to commemorate or honour them, or realising the brevity and value of life and making that springboard into some kind of major shift or change. Those who are able to find meaning tend to have a much easier time grieving than those that don't.'

Have I found meaning in my losses, the deep loss of Johnny, and what I have been through with my health? It is a question I am still in the process of answering, but I know that writing this book has helped me find meaning in some way and helped me to heal from my losses. Yet it is an ongoing process. I took to heart many things that Kessler writes in his important book on grief, but especially one of his sayings that 'pain is inevitable, but suffering is optional.'

I was in tremendous pain when Johnny died. That pain was a product of grief, which, as I wrote earlier, is the flipside of love. As Kessler writes, 'Suffering is the noise our mind makes around [that] loss, the false stories it tells because it can't conceive of death as random.' Learning to heal from loss doesn't mean that the loss didn't happen. It means that it no longer controls us and has changed us in some fundamental way.

And although that loss may no longer control us, that change does not always heal everyone. As David Brooks, an American writer and social commentator, sums up in his book *The Road to Character*: 'Recovering from suffering is not like recovering from a disease. Many people don't come out healed, they come out different.' And that is what grief does to us. It changes us. It transforms us. We may or may not be able to grow from it or become better people by having gone through that suffering, but we will be different people. As Kessler says, 'We often believe that grief will grow smaller in time. It doesn't. We must grow bigger. We must be the architects of our lives after loss.'

Three months after Johnny died, I visited his grave, which at the time did not yet have the gravestone erected on it. The magnitude of loss and grief I felt as I stood there is expressed in a poem I wrote that same evening.

April 2018

BY YOUR GRAVESIDE – AN ODE TO JOHNNY

When I stand by your graveside I feel an emptiness
Because I know you are not really there
You are everywhere, but not there
The clods of earth that cover your body are cold
They are waiting for the gravestone to be laid to mark your
    grave
The stake in the earth clearly states your name in bold
    Hebrew letters
But it is only your name not *you*
Not the man I knew and loved
That person no longer exists in a physical form
His body lies below the earth
Placed there three months ago
Your body lies there, Johnny
But where are you?
Where is the person I knew and loved?
My deepest need sometimes is that
I just need to know that you are in a good place
That you are watching over us
That you are in some way still a part of our world
But I know you are not part of our world in the physical
    sense anymore
You are part of our spiritual world
You are in a part of all of our hearts and minds
You, the very *alive* you, is still alive in our minds

You are alive in our souls and in our memories

When I stand by your graveside a deep sense of sorrow engulfs me

Sorrow for what I have lost

Sorrow for what I will no longer have in the days to come

Your touch, your voice, your presence beside me in good times and bad

You leaning over to place a gentle kiss on my cheek when I need cheering up

Your hug holding me when I need strength and I have needed so much of that in recent years

My sorrow could easily overwhelm me if I let it

But I cannot let it

There is too much at stake

For brief moments I open the crack and the sorrow pours out

In the tears rolling down my cheeks and the convulsions shaking my body

But then I regain my composure and close those cracks

Because a cracked vessel is vulnerable

And I need to try and be invulnerable

I need to try and be strong

I need strength and courage to take me forward for what I now face

But I do not face it alone

You have left me

But you have left me the most precious gift

Our children and their families

Our children are our legacy

And it is a legacy of love, devotion, unconditional support and continued strength

To face adversity with courage

I will need all of this from them to keep me going in the days to come

As I leave your graveside

With our four children by my side

I have every belief that God will shine His light upon us
And you will guide us to make the right decisions that will
    help us through what lies ahead
I leave your graveside but you will never leave me
You will be forever and ever in my heart
And in the hearts of all your family
Our love for you will never die

Johnny's death was the end of his lifetime, but not the end of our relationship, for that is eternal and this thought has helped me heal. It has allowed me to understand that dying is part of living, and I need to go on living without Johnny physically by my side. But I know he is still with me, eternally in my heart.

To quote Rachel Naomi Remen again, 'Grieving is not about forgetting. Grieving allows us to heal, to remember with love rather than pain. It is a sorting process. One by one you let go of the things that are gone and you mourn for them. One by one you take hold of the things that have become a part of who you are and build again.'

We grieve because we love. Grief is part of love. There was love in this world before our loss, there is love surrounding us now, and love will remain beside us, through all the life that is yet to come. Every kind of loss and its ensuing grief is made endurable by love, for love never dies; even in our darkest moments when we feel everything else is gone, love remains and continues. By understanding this, grief can be a pathway to open us up, heal us, and bring love and joy back into our lives.

Stepping
Stones

Lessons I have learnt about coping with loss and grieving

- Healing doesn't mean the loss didn't happen. It means it no longer controls us.

- Loss can be experienced any time when your planned future has been punctured by reality.

- Different stages of grief will be experienced at different times and processing them will help you to move forward.

- Grief is painful and accepting this means you must not deny your pain, which can be physical, emotional or spiritual.

- Accept that changes come in incremental steps as you begin to rebuild after loss.

- Reclaiming back a part of your former life after loss can help you heal.

- Finding some way of creating meaning in loss can help you move forward.

Pathway Three
Awareness of Love – Relinquishing Fear

'The greatest disease of mankind is the absence of love.'

— MOTHER TERESA

DIARY ENTRY: *May 2018*

There have been very few occasions since Johnny died when I have been left alone over Shabbat, as I am blessed to have my two sisters, my youngest son and many friends living nearby. But last Friday night I didn't feel up to going out. I wasn't feeling great and the weather was awful, so I decided to stay at home and was thinking deeply about all the Friday nights Johnny and I had spent together over the years. In recent times, several Friday nights had been spent in hospital or just the two of us at home, as I was not well enough to go out or have guests. Yet I remembered the happier Friday nights when our house would be filled with our children and many guests at our Shabbat table. Johnny was always the life and soul of those meals, and although he was not much help to me in the domestic realm, he was a wonderful host, full of entertaining stories and jokes. That's what I loved about him. That joie de vivre, that love for life, and I was blessed to have been the love of his life, as he was to me.

Writing these words, I remember so clearly what Johnny told me several years after we were married, about the first Friday night we spent together. It was the week after our wedding and Johnny was walking home from shul[1] trying to think what to talk about with me. We had been going out for over a year before we married, yet here he was thinking he didn't know how to keep me entertained for a few hours over a Friday night meal. Of course, in the end there was nothing to it; we just talked and talked, deepening our connection through words. But then I thought about the hundreds of hours we had spent in each other's company over the years, just the two of us, at home, on holiday, on long car journeys and, in later years, the interminable hours in hospital. There was no need for conversation, no need to say anything, for the love we had for each other didn't need any verbal expression. It was just being together side by side in each other's company that mattered, that meant more than anything else. Being there for each other, as the saying goes, 'in sickness and in health, until death do us part'…and eventually it did. But the love never dies. You can lose everything in life, but if you have loved someone that love will always be there.

Love is a supreme part of life in this world.

How many songs, books, plays and works of art are dedicated to the theme of love and romantic relationships? As the Beatles and countless other musicians have asserted over the years, 'Love is all you need.' A loving, open heart that is capable of giving and receiving love is the foundation of all good things in life, and it truly makes the world go round in more ways than we fully understand. Love is the cornerstone of healthy relationships and what makes human beings human. It is not just an emotion, feeling or experience; it is the very field in which all life lives. Love is also the source of profound healing.

---

1. Synagogue.

Human beings need to be with each other. Love is mentioned more than 500 times in the Torah,[2] and at the very beginning of creation, in the second chapter of *Genesis*, God declares: 'It is not good for man to be alone.' We redeem our solitude through our connection with an 'other'. And love is the most powerful connection there is – an invisible force that unites and expands us, and it is one of the most potent healing tools on the planet. But although love is instinctive in most human relationships, it is not always easy to engender. In many cases, love requires us to overcome our fears, to trust in a reality that is bigger than our challenges; sometimes it means we have to let go or let things be.

Love has the power to heal

Each day, as we wake up, we have a certain amount of mental, emotional and physical energy. Throughout the day we either spend or replenish that energy through our actions, which are guided by our emotions. One of the main themes running through literature I have read is that love and fear are the two key feelings that guide most of human emotion and behaviour. Take a look at the following examples.

LOVE	FEAR
gratitude, joy, acceptance, forgiveness, kindness, compassion, humour, happiness, trust, awe, optimism, admiration, serenity, amazement, inspiration, hope, sensitivity, freedom, radiance, passion, blessing, wholeness, peace, aspiration	anger, jealousy, anxiety, judgement, depression, despair, frustration, guilt, vengeance, hostility, contempt, disapproval, apprehension, humiliation, victimisation, pain, worry, sadness, shame, regret, doubt, insecurity, competition

---

2. The Jewish Bible, or Old Testament.

As I have come to understand, through my reading and my own personal experiences, emotions of love generate healing energy in the body while emotions of fear activate the stress hormones that lower the body's energy and negatively impact the immune system. If we deplete our energy through the emotions of fear, we have no energy to change our life or give to others. But if we raise our energy levels through actions that are guided by love, our world expands, for these elevated emotions are creative and selfless.

Physiologically, psychologically, physically and emotionally, your wellbeing is enhanced by your ability to generate the positive energy that comes from cultivating emotions of love. Emotions of love will give your body the impetus to heal from any type of trauma. Countless recorded experiences and proven scientific studies attest to this fact. That does not mean, though, that you cannot hold the opposing emotions of love and fear within you at the same time, for many of us do. What it does mean is what Gary Zukav writes in his book, *The Seat of the Soul*: 'When you choose to respond to life's difficulties with compassion and love instead of fear and doubt... you bring the aspects of a more balanced and harmonious level of reality into physical being.' Where you place your attention is where you focus on that which you want to receive, and where your energy gets directed. The body itself responds with a higher level of healing energy through emotions generated by love than those generated by fear.

Relinquishing fear

Fear is multifaceted and for so many of us, no matter how healthy a lifestyle we think we are living with regard to diet, exercise and relationships, our lives are subconsciously controlled by fear. Fear we are not good enough – whether it comes to our appearance, our lifestyles or our successes. By not being, doing or having enough, we reject who we are at that present moment. There is a fear that something is missing in our lives and that we are always falling short. And this fear leads to a whole gamut of other related emotions, some of which are listed above. Of course, there are times when fear is the most appropriate emotion. Fear and all the emotions associated with it are survival instincts, which should not be ignored, consciously or subconsciously, for long, because that will have a deeply detrimental effect on the body's immune system.

It has been shown in many studies that our minds are instinctively programmed for negativity. In fact, doctors refer to the brain's 'negativity bias', which was the survival mode that kept our bodies alert and in a state of preparedness in ancient times. It is what helped our ancestors survive dangerous and unpredictable environments. Professor John Cacioppo and neuropsychologist Rick Hanson, both working in America, found that this is still the case. Experiments observing the brain showed a greater surge of electrical neural activity to negative stimuli than to positive ones, suggesting that our attitudes are affected more by bad images or events than good ones.

In today's world we tend to focus on the more sensationalist 'bad' events in our lives, which stimulate all the emotions of fear as outlined previously, especially stress, which supresses the functioning of the immune system. Stress can also occur when you have expectations that are not met, or when your belief system and lifestyle don't match up – when you are not living as your authentic self.

There is another factor that can cause fear and stress, and that is living in uncertainty. Worry, anxiety and insecurity, which are all negative emotions of fear, rise to the surface if you are in an unstable environment where you do not know what will happen next. This could be something as serious as illness, unemployment or a bad relationship, or just the inability to plan ahead due to unforeseen circumstances. In today's world, stress and anxiety have become even more widespread with the Coronavirus pandemic, which has affected every aspect of our lives. Many people have had to contend with the uncertainty and fear that comes with lockdown, unemployment, furlough or attempting to work while homeschooling their children, as well as taking care of ageing parents or other vulnerable people who are self-isolating.

Through illness and grief, I have learnt that it is vital to try to relinquish the emotions that are caused by fear and cultivate the emotions that are guided by love. By relinquishing, I don't mean denying; I mean accepting they exist but then letting go of them. Holding on to these feelings keeps you stuck in the past rather than letting you live in the present moment. This is not easy. It takes courage and willpower, but the positive effects cannot be overemphasised.

But how is it possible to relinquish fears when they can be a genuine cause for concern, and even life-altering?

First, it's important to acknowledge that these fears exist within you. Accept they are there and although they can be overwhelming at times, you shouldn't feel guilty for having them. They are real and they are impacting your life. But in order to move forward, you have to let go of fear by accepting who you are and where you are at the present moment. Once you have accepted your feelings and calmed your mind, you can make space to cultivate emotions of love. It is in that space that you can nurture love, by pursuing all the associated emotions such as gratitude, joy, forgiveness and awe; they are the sources of positive energy that will help healing take place. Learning to live in the present moment is important, a lesson that meditation teaches us. When you focus on possible negative future scenarios, that is how fear seeps in.

Cultivating love

In the Torah, love is described not just in reference how humans interact with one another, but also in how God interacts with humans. In Judaism, the very foundation of the world is seen as being dependant on lovingkindness, as encapsulated in the Jewish concept of chessed.[3] Within Kabbalah, which is Judaism's

---

3. Lovingkindness.

esoteric, mystical tradition, chessed is one of the ten fundamental forces, the sefirot, that sustain the world. Chessed as love is seen as an inclination towards and an attraction to things, an opening up and a giving. Lovingkindness knows no restraint; it is love expressed as deed. Rabbi Lord Jonathan Sacks expresses this idea beautifully in his book To Heal a Fractured World: The Ethics of Responsibility.

'*Chessed* is the love that is loyalty, and the loyalty that is love. It is born in the generosity of faithfulness, the love that means being ever-present for the other, in hard times as well as good; love that grows stronger not weaker over time. It is love moralised into small gestures of help and understanding; support and friendship; the poetry of everyday life written in the language of simple deeds. Those who know it experience the world differently to those who do not … It is [a world] where trust is rewarded precisely because it does not seek reward. *Chessed* is the gift of love that begets love.'

Helping and loving others allows you to go deeper into yourself, to open up your heart, and in many cases to learn to love yourself through a sense of worthiness and commitment. In order to truly love others, you need to love yourself. I'm not talking about loving yourself in a narcissistic way but rather in an authentic manner so that your heart can fully open up and be able to love others and likewise accept their love too. And that means you need to accept yourself and find peace by understanding what brings meaning to your life. Learning to love and accept yourself for who and what you are will help you to deepen your relationships with others.

When I look back over my life through the lens of the above concept, I realise that so much of my healing has come from understanding the true nature of the relationships I had with myself and with members of my family. There were many different facets to these relationships and over the years they changed. The one thing they all gave me was the transcendent realisation that I was enveloped by love throughout my life. This was a force for healing. Yet our traditional concept of love is not always how it is played out in reality. It took a life's journey to see how love was at the centre of my personal struggles and healing and I want to share aspects of that here.

Love in my childhood

The love I was surrounded by ever since I was a young child was there underpinning the framework of my life without me even noticing it. It was something that I didn't think about in my childhood, since children tend to accept the circumstances they grow up in as the norm. They learn about relationships from the way they see adults interact, and don't question these interactions too deeply until they are exposed at some later point in their lives to a different type of dynamic. My parents did not always demonstrate their love physically or through words in my childhood; the love I received from them was never overt or gushing. We would get hugs from my mother, but love wasn't necessarily expressed in words. Rather, it was the quiet, secure feeling that they were there if I needed them. They were supportive and caring, rarely critical, but because we were not a family that talked about our feelings, or discussed issues in great debates, perhaps there was an element of my emotional maturity that didn't fully develop at the time.

Our home, though, was a safe and secure space for us to be who we wanted and needed to be. Their love was never predicated on us meeting their expectations. Such conditional love can engender fear in many ways. My parents never pushed us or vocalised their expectations for us to succeed; they allowed us to develop in our own ways. The flipside of that approach is that if you are not praised for what you do achieve, it can affect your self-esteem and feelings of self-worth. Maybe that was why I always worried about not being enough.

Although my mother worked full time throughout my childhood, I rarely felt I was lacking in her attention. For me it was the norm that she wasn't necessarily at home when I came back from school. The love I had from her was expressed in the warmth of her presence when she was there and in seeing her look after the family. But for my father it was different. He found it difficult to express love in a demonstrable way and now as an adult I understand better why this was. Having lost all his family in the Holocaust and having survived incarceration in several work and concentration camps, I believe his body may have healed from the physical scars, but I don't think his heart fully healed. I believe that in part it remained broken with its mental and emotional scars. Underneath the love that I know he had for us, I think he held a deep fear of losing his family again and this made him rein in his emotions and prevented him from showing us too much affection.

As a Holocaust survivor he hardly ever talked to us about his family life in Poland before the war. I believe that it was just too painful for him to talk about the physical loss of his family and his former life, as well as the suffering he experienced living through the hell of the Nazi camps. He wanted to shield us, his children, from this horrific knowledge. That he met my mother, fell in love, proposed two weeks later, eventually married and built a new family was nothing short of miraculous. There was a seed of love within him that survived. But looking back, maybe it was his fears for the future, combined with his losses in the past, that caused an inner stress to build up within him.

Still, I never witnessed my father display any hatred or desire for revenge for what he went through. My sister Zena, however, does remember several times when my father was distraught, but she is the eldest and I imagine she was more aware of the situation than I was at the time. To me, he was a sociable and honest man who kept his faith, practised his religion, and worked hard to give his family the security he lacked in his formative years. We were the family that he could not envisage ever having after the traumatic times he lived through. Each milestone in his life, from the birth of his three children to our weddings and eventual arrival of his grandchildren, was a miracle for him. He couldn't express his love in words, for that may have opened the floodgates for his emotions, but the tears streaming down his face at so many poignant moments attested to the fact that deep down his love was there, rising above the embers of his parents' and sisters' ashes and the fears that maybe he had tried to relinquish over the years. He died far too young at the age of sixty-seven, at a time when, in some ways, I was not emotionally mature enough, even at the age of thirty-five, to fully understand his life and his relationship with us.

I was discussing this recently with my sister Dina when I had a sudden epiphany about why our father may have found it difficult to show many of his emotions of pride and love. She mentioned the concept of *ayin hara*,[4] which in Judaism is an age-old notion that I suppose in today's terms we would call 'bad karma'. In a way, it encapsulates exactly the tension between the two emotions of fear and love, for *ayin hara* is the fear of tempting fate by expressing love too much; it is the fear that if you express or show your love or admiration publicly for someone or something, you can incite jealousy in a person hearing or witnessing this and they will be envious. But this does not even have to be a person, it could be the 'evil eye' of the universal force of God and the angels, in that you are tempting fate. It would be your pride that could cast negative energy and 'bad thoughts' towards that person you are praising or celebrating. As the saying goes: 'pride comes before a fall.'

This concept of *ayin hara* is rooted in ancient Jewish mystical thought and superstition, and my father with his eastern European background would certainly have been exposed to this in his upbringing. When I look back, I think that maybe that was why he never wanted to make a fuss about birthdays, anniversaries or any big event or achievement, and why, as much as he felt pride in his family, he would not express it openly. Superstitious customs remain to this day in several different religious traditions, with some people wearing a red thread or another type of accessory to ward off the evil eye. Through this they are trying to create some form of certainty to overcome their vulnerability.

Maybe my father's reluctance to express his feelings was also a sign of the times in which he lived. People then were not as emotionally open as they are now, and talking about feelings, especially

---

4. Literally, the evil eye.

among men, was uncommon. In the same way that illnesses were kept private out of a fear of being vulnerable, hiding one's emotions was likewise partly a defence mechanism, and perhaps for my father it was his defence against breaking down by being emotionally overwhelmed.

Growing up in the 1950s and '60s, children's feelings, and feelings in general, were not given much credence. The post-war generation just got on with it – and this attitude was reflected in many people's parenting methods. Most Holocaust survivors and so many of the refugees that made up my parent's circle of friends never had any form of counselling or parenting classes that are prevalent today. I don't think that our parents loved us any less than we as parents love our own children; it is just that one generation later, society has changed, and relationships are explored and expressed in different ways.

My personal love

When Johnny asked me to marry him, I initially turned him down. Our relationship had been the longest that I had had with any boy I had dated, but at the age of twenty-one I was still very young and in some ways quite immature. I had known Johnny for many years as part of my older sister Zena's circle of friends. In fact, the first time I set eyes on him was when he bounded into my life quite literally, as he fell down the staircase in our house at a meeting of Zena's Sinai group.[5] I must have been around thirteen or fourteen when Johnny and his good friend Eddie went to the top of the staircase and pretended to have a fight, punching each other and then ducking the blows. But finally, Eddie directed a blow at Johnny's stomach and he rolled down the entire staircase only to land on his two feet and bounce up. It was a great party piece and had everyone gasping with delight when they realised it was all a joke. Johnny was incredibly slim and supple in those days, and the

---

5. Local youth club.

image of him laughing as he picked himself up off the floor never quite left me.

Several years later we met again when he was the *rosh*,[6] in charge of running Sinai Junior Camp, and I was one of the *madrichim*.[7] But he was four years older than me and not in the same group of close friends and it would take another couple of years until I was in my final year of high school that we found ourselves mixing in the same crowd. He was always the one making jokes and laughing and it didn't go unnoticed that he was also rather good-looking. This was the time when I was thinking of taking a gap year and joining the Bnei Akiva Hachshara[8] scheme in Israel which was based at Kibbutz Lavi. Johnny had been on this scheme five years previously and had thoroughly enjoyed his year there, often saying it was the making of him. However, none of his close friends had been and he was therefore delighted to hear that I was considering going. We now had something in common and he encouraged me to join the scheme, going into great detail about all the amazing things that he had gained from his year there.

Little did I know it at the time, but it was this bond that would bring us closer and eventually lead to us dating. During that year, I wrote very long letters to him detailing my daily activities and feelings about being in Israel. Despite the fact that he warned me before I left that he was a terrible letter writer, he managed to write regularly and our correspondence deepened our friendship and regard for each other. When I returned from Israel, what had been a platonic relationship through our correspondence turned into a deeper one as we started dating and after a year he proposed. But there was something in me that was uncertain and not quite ready to make that commitment.

My life had been uncomplicated and relatively easy until that

---

6. Head counsellor.

7. Counsellors.

8. A particular gap year scheme organised by the Bnei Akiva international youth movement.

point, and I don't think I fully comprehended what it meant to be 'in love' and commit to a lifelong relationship. However, I did feel that Johnny and I had a physical attraction to each other, shared similar outlooks, came from similar backgrounds and had many similar experiences growing up in the same community. Most importantly, he made me laugh. He was the focus of the room whenever we got together with friends, he created the atmosphere, and that is an incredibly attractive quality. So yes, I did love him for all those qualities, but when it came to the point of actually saying yes, I suppose I got cold feet, but I cannot remember exactly what it was that I feared at the time. However, I knew that marriage was the expected norm in our circles and many of our friends were marrying and settling down, so finally after weeks of dithering I took the plunge and agreed to marry him.

Without a doubt, it was the best decision of my life, for although in some ways I was an emotionally immature twenty-one-year-old, Johnny and I really were soulmates. But it took me many years of marriage and four children to fully understand what a true soulmate is, how love between two people can uplift and create growth in each other, and in those around you. But being a soulmate does not mean you have to match in every area; Johnny and I were direct opposites in so many ways. The food we liked, the books and television programmes we preferred; I was the academic, he was the businessman; I was softer when it came to the children's upbringing and Johnny was much stricter. Some little habits we each had annoyed the other (if toothpaste tubes didn't now come with their caps attached I would still be leaving them off!), yet despite various arguments over the years, we respected and supported each other, learning and growing together.

Building love within a family

As you get older, you realise how much of a two-way process love is. With marriage, and if you are blessed with the eventual arrival of children, it becomes more than just two ways; it becomes a multifaceted arena for relationships to grow and for love to deepen.

It is not always recognised as such, for life is busy, complicated and often messy. But I was blessed. Although there were arguments between us (which family doesn't argue?), we had strong underlying foundations and the framework of love supporting it and we weathered it all.

Having been brought up in a family where love was an undercurrent – there but not explicitly so – and relationships were not discussed, I wanted to create my own style of parenting with Johnny, who used to discuss everything and anything with his parents. We were open with all our children about most things and used to spend many a family meal discussing different issues. Within our family, like so many others, the love between different family members varied in nature. In general, the love of a parent for a child is very intense, a fact that children don't always internalise until they themselves become parents. The relationship between mothers and daughters can be different to that of mothers and sons, and likewise between fathers and sons and fathers and daughters. It's not that a parent loves one child more than another – just that the love in that relationship has a different facet to it.

I am truly blessed to have four children: a daughter Tanya, then three sons, Avi, Natan and Baruch, who may look alike, but are all totally different in character. I have always argued that I love them equally and there are no favourites (despite Baruch claiming that Tanya is, as she is my only daughter!). The love I have for them is not based on their gender or position in the family, but in relation to different aspects of their character and therefore the relationship with each one is slightly different. Growing up, each child needed different things at different times, and although we gave them all boundaries as to what was acceptable and what was not, it was essential that they understood that our love for them was unconditional.

When Johnny and I married, our wedding invitation had a motif made up of the initials of our names shaped into a tree with two birds perched on the top. Little did we realise at the time that it signified everything one has to do when bringing up children.

When you bring up children, you have to do two things that seem contradictory: you have to give them roots, and at the same time you have to give them wings. The tree with its roots and the birds with their wings represent the two key issues of stability and freedom. Growing up, children need to know their roots, their background, where they come from. They also need to be given the freedom to go off and find their own place in the world, secure in the knowledge that those roots will remain in place, holding up the tree to which they can return, whenever they want to, after they have flown the nest. If you have given children a strong foundation of love from which to grow, they will create their own nests in which to nurture their young ones.

As they developed from young children into discerning adults, I accepted all my children for who they were, in the same way that I accepted Johnny for who he was when we married. When you marry someone you have to marry them for who they are, not who you want them to be.

Selflove and overcoming fear

My medical issues over the years, culminating in my cancer diagnosis, shone a light on the fact that I had never fully accepted myself for who I was. Even though I liked who I was growing up, there was an element of selflove missing, perhaps because love was not expressed openly by my parents. I realise that as a youngster I was constantly trying to please others and it is possible that this led me to fear so many things, which just multiplied when I became a parent.

I became both a worrier and a warrior. Worrying that I wasn't good enough, worrying about my children and family, about those around me, fearing failure in anything I undertook. And because of these fears, I slowly became a warrior. I don't mean this in a negative sense, in that I was at war with everything around me, but rather in the sense that I was trying to accomplish whatever I could in the best way possible. These character traits are discussed in greater detail in the next pathway, but within the context of this one, all these traits fall under the heading of fear. Even though I had a good and loving relationship with my husband, my children, my parents and my wider family and circle of friends, I realise now that, if I am being totally honest, it was a subconscious struggle to have to constantly prove myself worthy, and please everyone all of the time, even if at the time it didn't actually feel like that. Because my parents were not overbearing and closely involved in so many aspects of my life, I needed some sort of praise and reassurance from them for my efforts, which was not always forthcoming. Their love for me and pride in me as I grew up were there, of that I was somehow assured, it's just that it was not expressed at the time.

Rereading the above passages, I realise that I may come across as slightly ungrateful for what was genuinely a stable upbringing. Please understand me when I say I am exceptionally thankful for this, but I want to illustrate that even a person from a secure background, who really doesn't have big issues, can impose a subjective narrative onto reality. This in turn can 'create' conditions that tap into our fears and allow stress and worry to take over our inner world and cause untold damage to the physical body.

As serious illness overtook my life, and I could no longer take care of others, the people-pleasing side of my nature could not be fulfilled and I came to realise that people can love me for who I am rather than what I do. The deep love that Johnny, my children and so many members of my family and friends showed for me brought me back to who I truly am. They opened up the space which allowed me to internalise all the elements of love in my life, and this strengthened me even more.

The power of love

My longest inpatient stay during my cancer treatment was the two months I spent in hospital after my stem cell transplant. It was one of the most difficult periods in my life and there was much to fear before, during and after the operation. (Although operation is not quite the right word for it, since it's more of a procedure. The actual infusion of the donor cells is much like an ordinary blood transfusion.) It is the effects of the intense chemotherapy beforehand, designed to wipe out your entire immune system to prepare it for the donor cells, that creates the gruelling aftereffects that kick in days later. I remember my daughter Tanya sitting in my room watching me being hooked up to the tubes. What was amazing was how calm I was through the hourlong process. Tanya didn't quite believe me when I said that once the procedure started, I felt a sense of calm spreading through me. I had her next to me, my family nearby, and I knew that so many people around the world were reciting tehillim[9] for me at that precise moment, thanks to my cousin Cherry who had set up a refuah shlemah[10] WhatsApp group for me.

Somehow the energy of all that combined love was the stronger emotion that penetrated through to my soul, helping me to overcome the fear. Whereas fear can rob you of your energy, love helps to replenish it.

I was shut away from the world in a hospital room for over two months, where I was completely reliant on the incredible medical staff to look after me, together with members of my family who were at my bedside twenty-four hours a day. I was completely passive and dependent on others, and fear of surviving this difficult situation did penetrate into my consciousness at times. Yet throughout this period, the love of others towards me allowed that healing energy to reach deep inside, despite the fact that I often didn't know what day it was or lacked the strength to get out of bed after the transplant. I had the most amazing view of north London from my sixteenth-floor bedroom window at UCLH, but I couldn't even enjoy it for the first month I was there, seeing as I could barely lift my head off the pillow. It took many weeks for me to regain my strength and to be well enough to be discharged. It was then that the real deep fear set in. Some may say that I had become institutionalised, being so dependent on the medical team to care for me, that I feared leaving

9. Psalms.
10. In honour of a complete recovery.

the safety of the hospital to go home. I believe there is a lot of truth in that, as I realised that if something happened at home, I couldn't just press a buzzer for a nurse to come and help. So there was a real sense of fear, anxiety and worry.

However, something magical happened when I slowly walked back into my house on the day of my discharge, with Johnny by my side. It was a homecoming to where the deep love that had kept me going throughout the previous months was centred. This was my home, the place where together Johnny and I had built our lives and our family, and the love that I felt from my family gathered there to welcome me back home that day was overwhelming, casting out the fear and trepidation I had felt leaving the hospital.

But it didn't stop there. The following day I had what was the most emotional reunion of all. I had not seen my mother for the entire time I was hospitalised as the family felt it would be too distressing for her to be brought in her wheelchair up to the hospital, only to see me lying prostrate in bed, hooked up to all sorts of machines. And for the first month after the transplant I didn't even have the strength to speak to her on the phone. It was only in the few weeks before I was discharged that I managed to have a few short conversations with her. My illness had been a huge blow for her, and it was one of the worst days of my life when I had to break the news to her, years earlier. Since then, we tended to downplay my treatments to her, and thankfully I recovered quite quickly after each one, so I was able to keep up my regular visits to her. However, she knew about the transplant, and although she perhaps didn't realise just how precarious a procedure it was, she understood that I would be hospitalised for a while, and that we all hoped it would cure my cancer once and for all.

I will never forget the feeling I experienced finally seeing her after two months. I was still very weak and couldn't hug or kiss anyone because of the risk of infection. So we just sat down next to each other on the sofa. The intensity of the love that we shared during that hour together is something that is difficult to express in words. The emotion of love without any physical contact; the emotion of the love of a mother for a daughter and a daughter for a mother. Sixty years of love, of nurturing, of caring for each other, not always expressed in words but expressed in presence. Just like I wrote in my diary about the forty-year-relationship between Johnny and me.

Jack Kornfield, a renowned Buddhist teacher, captures this idea so beautifully in his book *The Art of Forgiveness, Lovingkindness and Peace*. 'Love creates a communion with life. Love expands us, connects us, sweetens us, ennobles us. Love springs up in tender concern, it blossoms into caring action. It makes beauty out of all we touch. In any moment we can step beyond our small self and embrace each other as beloved parts of a whole.'

Medical studies on the power of love

Love is the essence of the world we inhabit. But it is only in recent times that scientists have begun to understand the mechanics of the effects of love within the body through clinical studies, before which love was witnessed, experienced and understood but rarely measured within a scientific framework.

As an introduction, I want to tell you an extraordinary story. Anita Moorjani is one of the unique people who have had what is known as a near-death experience (NDE). She was suffering from stage four cancer, her body riddled with tumours, when she was admitted to hospital as her organs began to fail. She slipped into a coma and her husband and mother were told that it was too late to save her. Yet, as she records in her inspiring memoir *Dying to be Me,* she entered a state of pure bliss watching events unfold in her hospital room as if she was an observer outside of her own body. Many people who have had an NDE say that they have gone through similar scenarios, where they are aware of every detail of events happening to them, but they view it as an outsider, feeling no attachment to their physical bodies, which in most cases are severely compromised and for all intents and purposes seen by the doctors as no longer able to support viable life. And it is at that precise moment when they experience a profound insight that remains with them when they eventually return to their physical bodies. With Anita, the feeling she experienced was one of being encompassed by pure unconditional love, bathed in an energy that was healing with a true sense of belonging, of being home. After reawakening from her coma, to the astonishment of all the doctors, her entire body completely healed and within five weeks she was discharged from hospital.

Other accounts of NDEs relate to heavenly experiences where the person realises that all that matters for their soul is that they have undertaken acts of unconditional kindness in their lives, elements of love that have transcended everyday life. Anita's extraordinary story of her healing relates to the knowledge she gained through understanding that she was unconditionally loved. She realised that the underlying cause of her cancer was the many aspects of fear that had pervaded her life since a small child. And what cured her body was the recognition, through her NDE, that she did not need to do anything to be loved; that she was loved unconditionally just by being. As she writes in her book: 'My life was driven by fear – of displeasing others, of failing, of being selfish, and of not being good enough ... Since my NDE I don't feel I came back to *accomplish* anything. I only came back to *be*. Because of this everything I (now) do comes from love.'

So much of what we go through in life is driven by the necessity to *do*. How often are we allowed just to *be*? Just being ourselves allows us to process who we are, freeing up our inner energy to show us the possibilities of what we can achieve and become. Although my childhood was totally different to Anita's, reading her story made me think deeply about the changes I have experienced since becoming ill and then losing Johnny. In the same way that Anita describes her new perspective on life, living with unconditional love, I too have felt that my outlook has changed in a fundamental way. It is all the emotions of love that now guide so many of my decisions and actions. I have realised that I don't need to do anything to prove myself and my worthiness. It is enough to just be. So many of my fears from the past could have contributed to the underlying causes of my cancer. And as I wrote earlier, fear and all the emotions associated with it drain the body of its vital energy force.

Dr Joe Dispenza, whose ideas I discuss in greater detail in the following pathway, has conducted groundbreaking research into how your thoughts create your reality. His books are fascinating and for me, learning how our emotions are the energy pathways through which the genes in our bodies can be reprogrammed made enormous sense as I reflected back on my experiences over the years. I began to understand how the elevated emotions of love transmit higher frequency signals, whereas limited emotions such as fear, worry and anxiety create lower frequencies which deplete the body and particularly the immune system. He cites numerous examples of people who suffered from a variety of medical conditions and who, through reprogramming their thoughts towards the elevated emotions of love, have healed not only from their symptoms but in many cases have rid their bodies entirely from chronic diseases that have been present for many years.

After reading his books, I attended one of his seminars and over the past year I started to practise his meditations on a weekly basis. They have been very useful in helping me overcome certain mental blocks and achieve a better understanding of how attending to my emotional state can improve my wellbeing. Dr Dispenza has conducted many scientific studies including brains scans and blood tests on people as they create the emotions associated with love, and the results demonstrated how thoughts affect the body and improve the functioning of the immune system. He is passionate about giving scientific proof about how positive emotions and thoughts can help transform people's physical and mental health. He calls this 'information to transformation'. In the paradigm with which I have framed much of this book, it can be seen as the internalisation of experiences to create transformation and healing.

But like everything I write about in this book you have to be open to the ideas presented to you. As Dr Dispenza writes, the suggestibility of something doesn't mean it is 'something that all of us could do voluntarily on command… [because it] combines three elements: *acceptance, belief* and *surrender.* The more we accept, believe and surrender to whatever we are doing to change our internal state, the better the result we can create.' And this isn't just an intellectual process: 'the emotional component is the key in this experience.'

Love will triumph

Did I really need to get ill and lose my husband to understand the true nature of love and its power to heal? Did I really hold on to so much fear in my younger years that it was the cause of so much stress in my life? I cannot answer these questions, but I do know that looking back on all that I have experienced has allowed me to reframe my perspectives and understand how precious love is and how harmful it can be to hold on to fear. To know that you are held with love inside someone's heart is one of the most priceless gifts you can possess. There is a deep sense of love and belonging that is a basic need of all women, men and children. It attests to the fact that your souls and theirs are connected in the infinite field of energy that is part of the universal soul of mankind. Much of the latest work in neuroscience and epigenetics focuses on the idea that the more we are connected to others through our positive emotions, the more healing can occur in our bodies. We cannot see this connection for it is not quite the same as being 'connected' through technology like FaceTime, but just as we cannot see the waves of energy that transmit through our phone signals and radio waves, it is there. And there is an enormous healing effect of opening your heart to this energy.

When Johnny died, I knew that it was his physical body that had died, not his soul, for that is eternal, and that is where his love continues to transmit to me, giving me courage to continue to go forward with my life. The souls of all of those whom I have loved but are no longer physically present in my life – my husband, my parents, my parents-in-law, aunts, uncles, grandparents and friends – are out there. And there are moments when I know that the connection is reignited in another realm when I think about a particular person, such as on their *yahrtzeit*,[11] or reflect on something that reminds me of them. These connections exist not just with souls that are no longer attached to physical bodies, but with each and every living person. We are connected through our emotions, and the emotion of love is one of the strongest connections of all. Love is enduring, unconditional and what truly makes the world go around. So become aware of love in your life, and be guided by it, so you can let go of your fears. Then hopefully you will begin to heal.

Stepping  Stones

Lessons I have learnt about becoming aware of love and relinquishing fear

- Love has the power to heal through the positive emotions it engenders in the body.
- Generating these emotions can help to upgrade the body's immune system.
- Learning to love yourself allows you to truly open yourself up to being loved and loving others.
- Fear and its associated emotions deplete the body of vital energy and stimulate stress hormones.
- Fear can arise from perceived inadequacies in ourselves, when we feel we are not enough or do not have enough.
- Living with uncertainty can be one of the major causes of fear, which initiates stress.
- It is important to acknowledge your fears but then let go of them as much as possible.

---

11. Commemorating the day of a person's passing.

Pathway Four

Turning Thoughts into Reality –
The Power of Your Mind

'Life isn't about finding yourself. Life is about creating yourself.'
— GEORGE BERNARD SHAW

DIARY ENTRY: *December 2014*

Last week I was driving behind a white van that had a sticker on the back asking: 'How am I driving?' followed by a tele-phone number to call. Does anyone ever call the number when the person driving the vehicle does something wrong? Does it make you question your own driving ability? I have often seen these stickers and thought, 'Well, the person must think they are a good driver if they are prepared to have someone check up on them.'

But what about if we as individuals were to pin signs on ourselves asking 'How am I doing?' Would our family or friends report to us if they saw something was wrong? Would we be able to answer them truthfully? I am not sure how I would answer that question at the moment, for I honestly don't know how I am doing, not just physi-cally getting through each day, but what I am doing to get through each day now they have found out I have a genetic mutation which means most treatments are not likely to be as effective for me as for someone without this mutation. Not great news. I am not sure how the thoughts swirling around in my head will ever settle down or how I will be able to control them to feel better. I will try to carry on being positive, but it is hard as I really don't know what the future holds for me. I suppose only time will tell because I certainly can't.

Is the idea of mind over matter really so simple? Is it true that if you think deeply enough about something it will manifest itself? I have always believed that your thoughts become your reality; if you change your mindset and attitude, you can change your perspective, which then becomes your reality. I have previously written about how people with a more positive attitude tend to fare better in many situations. In my mind, it doesn't necessarily mean that everything they want to come about will happen. It just means that they will cope better with whatever does happen. But as my cancer journey progressed, I was to discover much more about the mind-body connection and how what was once inexplicable has now been investigated and proven scientifically. I was about to understand exactly how the mind *can* change body chemistry; how thought itself is an unmanifested emotion and once we embrace it emotionally it can become real, therefore creating a new reality.

Over the years, as my cancer became more complicated, and I was trying to cope with increasingly intensive treatments, I had to constantly reinforce in my mind the fact that I wanted to beat the odds. I wanted to survive. I would get through whatever ghastly treatment was next on the horizon and move forward. I wanted to be what Bernie Siegel described as an 'exceptional patient'. But unfortunately, the cancer kept returning after each treatment. This happened six times after different forms of chemotherapy, immunotherapy and even a stem cell transplant. Each time the tests showed the cancer had come back, I kept trying to remain positive, but it was becoming increasingly difficult.

I was lucky in that my wonderful doctor, Claire Dearden,

maintained an air of positivity while always being realistic in managing our expectations. She kept up our optimism with talk about finding new treatments, working with the doctors and exploring new approaches. I tried to keep my thoughts focused on where I wanted to be once I was well and over my cancer. I had learnt this technique from my sister Zena's stepdaughter, Nicola Behrman, who helped me with visualisation, meditation and other techniques that opened me up to connect with my spiritual and emotional side and understand how to tap into the well of energy deep inside me that I needed to help heal my body.

Years ago, the breathing and relaxation sessions at the end of each of my yoga sessions had started me on the meditation pathway, so I understood its benefits. The problem was that most of the time, when my life was on a relatively even keel, I did not utilise its full potential and I didn't meditate regularly. This all changed once I was diagnosed with cancer. I used many of the meditation and breathing techniques I had learnt to help me through everything from having to lay completely still through CTs, MRIs, spinal injections and bone biopsies, to combating post-chemotherapy nausea.

Many medical doctors would not think of suggesting meditation, for although they know a huge amount about the body, medical procedures and treatments which may cure disease, they know less about how energy in the body connects the heart and brain, creating physical changes and how the mind can direct healing. I was about to discover far more in a book that changed my whole understanding of the mind-body connection, as it detailed the science behind so many studies showing how the mind really can change the body's chemistry.

I had reached a decisive point in my cancer journey. Nine months after going through an extremely gruelling stem cell transplant, my cancer returned. The doctors recommended a top-up from my transplant, which in simple terms means they give you more chemotherapy and a further infusion of the original cells used in the transplant. After this took place, I had a short period of breathing space when my scan showed me to be in remission, so Johnny and I took the opportunity to fly out to Israel to see our children and grandchildren. And it was at this point that the biggest tragedy of our lives happened – when Johnny died suddenly after contracting pneumonia while we were there. I cannot say for sure that the shock of his death and the ensuing trauma was the reason my cancer returned yet again, but it did after four months.

My family and I decided to have one more try with a second top-up, but at the same time we began exploring further options should the cancer return again. We had contacted hospitals in America where they were seeing good results with a new, groundbreaking treatment called CAR-T cell therapy, which at the time I could not get access to in the UK. This was very timely as my lymphoma resurfaced yet again several months after the second top-up. As I mentioned earlier, we were very fortunate to find Dr Fred Locke and access this new treatment at the Moffitt Cancer Centre in Tampa, Florida. Just before I left for a two-month stay in Florida, Nicola recommended I read Dr Joe Dispenza's book, *You Are the Placebo*. This book was to be a revelation and a guiding force for me. It broadened my whole outlook on how I could find wellness in my illness, through focusing my mind and changing my thought patterns. I had started visualisations and emotional conditioning work months earlier and this book placed the whole topic within an understandable framework. It was fascinating reading, detailing the performance of placebos in trials and their success in healing patients of their illnesses, as well as showing the nocebo effect of negative thoughts.[1] Through numerous studies, Dr Dispenza showed that 'in exactly the same environment, those with a positive mindset tend to create positive situations, while those with a negative mindset tend to create negative situations.'

The whole premise of Dr Dispenza's book is that you can reverse many chronic conditions by believing in a placebo. And

---

1. The nocebo effect is when having negative expectations about a medical procedure causes it to affect the patient more negatively than it otherwise would have done.

the enormous number of scientific studies that he references show that placebos in trials often have the same – and sometimes even better – results than the original drug being tested. He poses the question, 'Is it possible to teach the principles of the placebo and, without relying on any external substance, produce the same internal changes in a person's health?' and then goes on to illustrate that it is. He goes into great detail as to how the thoughts and feelings that shape your attitudes and beliefs are accessed from your past experiences to become the template for your future. He explains how, by changing the original thought patterns and attaching these to heightened positive emotions, the body's chemistry can be changed in the future.

It was what Dr Bernie Siegel and others had noticed years earlier but didn't yet have the scientific experiments to back up. But now there were studies with real results. How this all works at a cellular level is explained in the book. Not everyone may agree with Dr Dispenza, or find it within themselves to go down this path, but in my opinion, it is a truly scientific theory that has been carefully thought through and backed up by numerous controlled experiments. And I have found that it has worked for me as I've realised that in some way I can create a new reality and new state of being by changing my thoughts, actions and feelings.

Some of the spontaneous remissions from all sorts of diseases that Dr Dispenza witnessed in his workshops were remarkable. He argues against genetic determinism (the idea that nature is responsible for everything, rather than nurture), saying we are programmed to think we are victims of our biology. However, 'fewer than 5% of the world's population are born with some genetic condition – like type 1 diabetes or Down's syndrome … The other 95% of us who develop a condition acquire it through lifestyle and behaviours.' The whole new science of epigenetics explores how the DNA in our cells is controlled by factors outside of the cell, for example, our lifestyles or the environment we live in. And one of the major environmental factors causing epigenetic change is stress, which can have a devastating effect on the body.

Letting go of stress

For years I lived a life where I put myself through untold stress. I was the eternal worrier. Johnny often commented that I was forever worrying about everything, very often before anything had even happened. He would say: 'What's the point of worrying before there is anything to worry about?' Of course, he was right, and I tried to counter his comments by saying that I was merely thinking about things rather than worrying about them. But it was as if my brain had internalised the old Jewish joke: 'Start worrying. Details to follow.' My father was also a worrier, which is no wonder given his background, and I always thought that I must have inherited his 'worrying gene'. But I never realised that I could change this inherited pattern.

Dealing with worry, anxiety and stress takes its toll, whether these are money or job worries, health or relationship issues, or just trying to continually prove your worth to others and to yourself.

What's interesting is that even though I have always been a worrier by nature, I have been blessed for most of my life not to have deep issues to worry about. I had a happy marriage with four great if not sometimes challenging children (who doesn't have challenging parenting moments?), wonderfully supportive and caring parents, in-laws and siblings, plenty of friends and relatively good health. I lived in a comfortable home and my husband's business was able to support the family. So why did I worry so much? It's a good question and I honestly don't have an answer. All I can say is that for many years I put myself under unnecessary stress for a variety of reasons: childrearing, ageing parents, trying to juggle work and voluntary charity commitments, forever feeling there are not enough hours in the day for what I wanted and needed to achieve, trying to please everyone all the time and feeling that I *did* need to achieve. So yes, maybe it was self-induced stress, but that can happen to anyone.

I have a wonderful magnet on my fridge that says: 'Worry is like a rocking chair. It will give you something to do but it won't get you anywhere.' The wisdom of some fridge magnets should not be so quickly dismissed. As our children grew up it was a running joke amongst our family and friends that I was always the one providing endless amounts of food just in case anyone got hungry whenever we went out; sun cream was forever slapped on and no swimming allowed for at least half an hour after food. And these were the minor issues; don't ask what I felt like when I watched the children head off to their first sleepaway camp, their first holiday away with their friends and then their gap years abroad. So yes, I was constantly worrying about the welfare of my family in every situation. But that's what so many parents do, although it is generally interpreted as 'caring' rather than 'worrying'. But I realise now that even as a young child I worried about things in the sense that didn't want to be a bother to anyone. Perhaps this feeling stemmed from a lack of self-worth, but I think this was more to do with a sense of wanting to please everyone all the time, which can also be an underlying cause of stress.

I have memories of shopping trips with my mother and sisters when they would go off and choose the prettiest and often the most expensive dresses in the shop and I would just choose the nearest and cheapest dress and say 'I like this one,' just to make things easy for my mother. Often when I was asked what I would like, whether it was a type of food or a place to go to, I would answer with: 'Whatever you would like.' I am not trying to make myself out to be some sort of 'goody two shoes', it's just how I remember those experiences as I look back, trying to make sense of it all, to see how it affected my personality in later years. So yes, maybe that's where my worrying nature was nurtured. I was trying to please everyone; I didn't want to be a burden or take too much from anyone. Nature or nurture? That is an age-old question and, as I mentioned earlier, there is no doubt that one's genetic makeup does affect one's personality. Of course, the genes we inherit from our parents and grandparents dictate to a degree our bodies' chemistry. If we do not change our thought patterns to change that chemistry, the patterns of behaviour will just continue repeating themselves.

There is another theme here, which I am not going to go into in depth, but I feel it is worth mentioning, and that is the fact that I am a middle child. In 1964, doctor and psychologist Alfred Adler developed a theory about the importance of birth order in personality development. Since then, there has been a lot of research on the effect of birth order on a person's personality, but much of this has produced conflicting evidence. However, two of the traits often attributed to being a middle child, known as 'middle child syndrome', do strike a chord with me. First, middle children tend to be peacemakers in adult life. Second, they hold themselves up to impossibly high standards, thinking that whatever they do is not good enough. The reasons for this are complex and not a topic for discussion here, but suffice to say it's possible that there are elements of my personality that developed because I was sandwiched between an older and a younger sister. By age ten, I had grown almost a foot taller than my older sister and was constantly mistaken as the eldest child in the family by people who did not know us well. I was extremely conscious of my height at that age, and it didn't help that in primary school, when our class had to line up in the playground in height order, I was always stuck at the back. I am not sure if this awkwardness played out in our relationships as sisters at the time, but like most siblings we had periods when we got along and other times when we fought with each other. As children, we were not always the best of friends, but once we married and had our own children, our relationships changed and intensified. Today, Zena and Dina are my closest friends, and I could not imagine life without them.

Worrier and warrior

Being a worrier for so many years turned me into a warrior. I was constantly worrying I wasn't good enough and then tried hard to prove I was. This applied to schoolwork, exams and many other areas of my life. If I would conduct an analysis of myself I think deep down the drive I have to always give 110% of myself has its roots in my background.

A friend of mine, who comes from several generations of English

Jewry, once commented to me that she had noticed something special about the children of Holocaust survivors. She felt that many of her friends with this background were very driven in what they did and were the ones who were often spearheading all kinds of different initiatives. I think this is a plausible observation because I have read some of the literature about the generation born to Holocaust survivors and it strikes a chord. For me personally, I think there was an element of feeling the need to prove myself worthy not only of my namesake (my father's sister who died in the Holocaust and who I am named after), but of giving validity to my father's survival. The fact that my father named his three daughters Zena, Mindy and Dina after his three sisters who were murdered by the Nazis meant that he lived every day with a reminder of his loss, but for us as his children, we each took a different meaning from it. Whereas I felt I had to prove myself worthy of my namesake, Zena said she often felt that she carried the burden of survivor's guilt. Dina she says she was very aware of being a Holocaust survivor's daughter and felt quite driven by this.

My parents were not pushy or overbearing people and in no way demanded anything of me or my siblings, either academically or socially, and certainly the legacy of the Holocaust in our family was never discussed. The pressure came from within to prove that I was worthy. Thankfully I did do relatively well in my academic studies and went to university completing both a bachelor's and master's degree, but still the worry always lingered in the background that I wasn't good enough.

The detrimental effect of stress

It is sometimes hard to trace the origin of an illness, but likely candidates such as smoking, being overweight, having bad eating habits and other environmental factors are often cited as causes. However, it is known that living with stress is certainly a major factor in so many of today's diseases, whether chronic or acute. I cannot pinpoint when and how my cancer may have developed, but a few years before I was diagnosed, I went through a period of extreme stress, unlike anything else I'd ever experienced in my life. For over six months, I worked on a project that was so stressful that I barely slept during that time. I had reached a low point in my life which lasted for several months and, despite the ultimate success of the project, it had taken a huge toll on me and my health. My cancer diagnosis years later and subsequent treatment was without doubt the biggest wakeup call for me to face up to the fact that I had put my body through years of stress and it was time to sort myself out.

Stress, worry and anxiety produce, amongst many other things, an increase in levels of cortisol in the body, which can create havoc within the immune system. It seems that humans were programmed to deal with short-term stress in the form of a fight-or-flight response to danger. Once the danger passed, the body would return to its normal resting state. But in the modern world, we never seem to cut off from the stresses in our lives and so, what was supposed to be a short-term chemical response within our bodies has become long term, with damaging results.

Dr Dispenza describes a study in Ohio where they found how stress affects the healing of skin wounds. Researchers reported that the wounds of stressed patients took 40% longer to heal. And there are many similar experiments that highlight the negative effects of stress on the healing mechanisms in the body. Furthermore, Dr Dispenza maintains that 'as we keep making stress hormones we create a host of highly addictive negative emotions including anger, hostility, aggression...frustration...fear, insecurity, guilt, depression and powerlessness...When we focus our thoughts about bitter past memories or imagined dreadful futures...we prevent the body from regaining homeostasis.'

When we lose control over our lives, and things don't go according to plan, the result is a whole gamut of emotions that are primarily associated with fear and stress. During my cancer treatment, I felt stressed not only because of my fear of the illness, but because of its unpredictability. I never knew if treatments would work and if they did, how long my remission would last. I had no control over my future, in the same way that so many people suffer now with a loss of control over their lives due to the Corona pandemic.

DIARY ENTRY: *January 2016*

As a young child I loved going to the funfair. It was a special treat where the throwing of wooden hoops or ping pong balls usually ended up with a goldfish or two being brought home in a plastic bag. These were then hastily transferred to the glass bowl only recently vacated by the previous year's expired goldfish. I loved the dodgems too, where at the tender age of eight I was allowed to drive a moving car and bash into all the other cars. But there was one ride I never went on. After just a single experience which left me dizzy, nauseous and distinctly out of sorts, I never again attempted a ride on a roller coaster.

It is perhaps ironic then that these past few years have been one long roller coaster ride. From the time of my cancer diagnosis until the present day, when I am about to start yet more treatment, there have been so many ups and downs, I sometimes feel like I am a pawn on a snakes and ladders board. How can I plan anything when my life seems to depend on the roll of a dice? Monthly blood tests, treatment yes or no, another infection, more medication, is my scan clear or not? My hopes are raised and then dashed again, and like the carriage on a roller coaster my emotions go up and down and I never know what waits in store around the next bend.

After enjoying a nine-month remission, the cancer has returned. The ups of being able to travel, get back into some kind of normal routine, actually plan to do things, are now weighed down by the downs of being returned to my little medical box which encases me in a world of doctors, hospitals and ongoing treatments. This time, it's a new biological therapy which my doctor has great hopes for. Not necessarily for a cure, but it might buy me some precious time with a period of remission.

So yes this roller coaster ride, with its chemotherapy pit stops on the way, often leaves me feeling dizzy, nauseous and distinctly out of sorts, fearful for the future, and there is no way to get off.

Carl Jung called anxiety 'fear spread thin', which is a wonderful depiction of what so many people experience in their everyday lives, and even more so during Corona. Even when restrictions ease, the sense of 'unease' is palpable. A multimillion-pound industry has grown up around the need to deal with stress in the modern world. From luxury spas that promise to detox your mind and body to the profusion of psychotherapists, psychologists, self-help gurus and thousands of books available on the topic, not to mention Big Pharma and the plethora of drugs prescribed by doctors for stress, anxiety and depression. All these methods, however, are only successful if they are not treated as quick fixes but are accompanied by a deep awareness of the causes of stress and a willingness to change your mindset. If a person is in denial about the source of their stress, they won't have the strength to deal with it.

Many of the healing pathways that I have described in this book have not only helped me cope with the stress of my illness and bereavement but have also helped me understand what causes stress in the first place. Reading about the different mechanisms at work within the body that can be altered through meditation and other techniques has helped me to create new ways of thinking and envision a new, better reality in which I can go forward. In order to heal, you need to change the way you think and this is not easy; anyone who has gone through the process of trying to change their mindsets will understand this. But if you recognise just how much power you truly possess within your mind, and you have the will to do it, anything is possible.

Stepping
Stones

Lessons I have learnt about turning thoughts into reality and the power of the mind

- Your mindset and attitude create your perspective and shape your reality.

- Stress is one of the most damaging things that can affect the immune system.

- External situations can create stress or it can be self-induced from thought patterns and behaviour of individuals.

- Your thought patterns govern your body chemistry to by changing these you can affect your emotions which can create physical changes in the body.

- An inclination to constantly please others may take away from your own selfcare.

- Humans are built to deal with short-term, not long-term stress. Learning to deal with stress requires work.

- You are never stuck – patterns can always be changed.

Pathway Five

Wisdom of Your Soul –
Emotions of Your Heart

'*You can't heal what you can't feel.*'

— DAVID KESSLER

DIARY ENTRY: *October 2017*

Three weeks ago, I felt that I couldn't carry on anymore. I had reached my lowest point. Everything had gone wrong and I almost gave up. I can't even write down the emotions I felt. The whole story behind one of my darkest episodes since my stem cell transplant last year is a long one, but suffice to say that having an emergency admission to the wrong hospital for a ten day stay over Rosh Hashana,[1] being treated for an infection without all my notes or usual medical team in attendance, was a complete nightmare and had a serious effect on my mental wellbeing that even the period of my transplant did not induce.

The light at the end of the tunnel was truly fading. Yet somehow I pulled myself out of it. I just took one day at a time, noting any incremental progress. I kept telling myself that the healing I need will eventually come not just from

---

1. Jewish New Year

my doctors and the medical procedures I am going through. It will require a deep inner resolve as I need to work on it myself and listen to that inner voice that can guide me through it all. For healing is a triangle where the input has to come from three different arenas – from the doctors and the medical profession, from God, and from the person themselves. I want to get better, I need to feel I will get better and I need to open up to all those around me that are supporting me, praying for me to get better. I feel their love and support in so many ways and am eternally grateful for that healing energy coming my way.

In Judaism it is customary to insert in one's daily prayers a passage to pray for those who are seriously ill. It is very significant that when praying to God for the recovery of a named person, we ask for a healing of both 'soul and body', with the soul coming before the body. Having a healthy soul is a precursor to having a healthy body. Since going through the challenges of both physical illness and the mental anguish of bereavement, I have come to understand in a much deeper sense how a healthy soul, with its own wisdom, can lead to physical improvements in the body.

We are not aware of our soul in the same way we are of our body. As Rabbi Adin Even-Israel Steinsaltz, one of the great Talmudic scholars, elucidates in his book, *The Soul*: 'We are aware of most of our visible body parts, but are far less aware of our kidneys and livers and other organs that are hidden inside our bodies. We often become aware of our soul in the same way we become aware of our body's inner organs; when we suffer illness or experience pain in one of them... Often, the soul, or the message it relays, reaches us not as an epiphany but as a disturbance. Our inner reality is exposed when normal, natural consciousness is disrupted... Every fluctuation in our lives calls upon us to search for its source.'

Where the soul resides

But do you ever stop to think where your soul resides in your body? Do you ever stop to think at all about your soul? Is it located in your heart or is it part of the thinking brain? The expression 'soul-searching' doesn't mean you should physically locate where your soul is, but rather examine your motives and ask yourself what drives you to a particular course of action; what is the correctness and meaning of those actions and how impactful are they in a wider context? It provides the framework for purpose and meaning in your life. Does this come from the knowledge stored in our brains or is it something deeper, part of heart wisdom?

I have done a lot of soul-searching as I faced my challenges, but in a sense it has been not so much an examination of my motives as a search to comprehend what my soul connects with and understand how finding the answers could help my healing. This is not an especially religious search, more a spiritual quest to know and understand my authentic self, my place in the world and my interconnectedness with everyone around me. I am blessed that I have had the time and space to do this. At this stage in my life I have no young children or elderly parents who depend on me and whose routines I have to work around. Ever since my cancer diagnosis, I have not been in paid employment and my time has been my own. But even if you are busy and your days are filled, a crisis often forces you to question how you live your life and evaluate your priorities. It's no wonder that when one comes to a low point in one's life it is often referred to as 'the dark night of the soul'.

Your brain is the analytical, rational part of your body and your heart is said to carry your emotions and desires. Most people believe it is also the place where your soul resides. As I was searching for many different answers during my journey, I came across a book written over thirty years ago by Gary Zukav, *The Seat of the Soul*, and many of his ideas spoke to me on a deep level. It was a groundbreaking book at the time; he discusses how the deepest human values are found not in the physical reality of our five senses, but in something much deeper called the multisensory level, where your soul 'is not a passive or theoretical entity that occupies a space in the vicinity of your chest cavity... [rather it is] a positive, purposeful force at the core of your being. It is the part of you that understands the impersonal nature of the energy dynamics in which you are involved, that loves without restriction and accepts without judgement. This energy dynamic or karma... governs the balancing of energy within our system of morality... serving humanity as an impersonal and universal teacher of responsibility.' In essence, Zukav's idea is that you receive from the world what you give it. It is the understanding that the road to your soul is through your heart.

This thought resounded deeply with me as I navigated my challenges, and I started to explore the ways I had successfully coped in certain situations. From the very beginning, since I first heard my diagnosis, I tried not to succumb to fear, even though it is a natural reaction when hearing that you have a life-threatening illness. Perhaps I wanted to protect those around me so I did not allow myself to make 'heavy weather' of my diagnosis. My inner self guided me to try to remain positive, which was easier at the beginning since my cancer was thought to be nonaggressive and, although not curable, certainly treatable. Consciously choosing your intentions, such as trying to remain positive, creates a pathway for your soul to focus its attention, and this will shape your experiences. As Gary Zukav says, 'The intention behind an action determines it effects, every intention affects both us and others, and the effects of intentions extend far beyond the physical world... [for] every intention sets energy into motion, whether you are conscious of it or not.' This has sometimes been referred to as the 'butterfly effect,' a phrase coined by Edward Lorenz in the 1960s as part of chaos theory, where one small incident can have a big impact in the future.

The Hebrew word for intention, *kavanah*, is often used in association with the performance of a good deed, a *mitzvah*, and especially to prayer. Rabbi Abraham Joshua Heschel, one of the great spiritual teachers of the twentieth century, maintains that the purpose of Jewish practice is the transformation of the soul. If one doesn't have the correct intention when carrying out good deeds, it might have a positive effect on the world, but it will leave the doer of that deed unaffected. Where you focus your intention is where the body's energy is directed. If the intention is made with love, then that intention will raise the energetic level of the body and its surroundings, creating what one could call good karma. But if the intention is based on fear, then the energy is of a lower frequency, which is depleting and creates negativity.

As I discussed earlier, there are now scientific ways to prove that your intentions can become your reality, and this is how the soul manifests its wisdom. The field of quantum physics has opened up new areas of research into the heart-mind connections. Max Planck, a founding father of quantum physics, explained his thoughts about the nature of matter in the 1940s. He describes how matter exists by virtue of a force, and behind that force must be a conscious and intelligent mind, which is the matrix of all matter. Some might call this intelligent mind God, others a universal force, but it wasn't until recently that science, psychology and the ancient wisdoms came together to formulate a whole new understanding of just how this works in relation to connecting all life within a matrix that is a universal field of energy.

I was first introduced to these ideas at a seminar I attended featuring Dr Joe Dispenza. There was another fascinating speaker that day, Gregg Braden, whose book *The Divine Matrix* discusses in great detail how through this matrix, the heart and brain connect on an emotional level. He is one of the pioneers in this field, bridging science and spirituality, and he has shown that achieving heart-brain coherence has been scientifically proven to release healing chemicals into the body. He examines the twenty keys of conscious creation which open up all fields of possibility to transform our lives. The emotions we experience are the key, and it is through our emotions and our heart wisdom that we can change our body chemistry. Gregg Braden has been working for years with an organisation called the HeartMath institute, which has been developing scientifically validated tools that help people to reduce stress and increase life satisfaction, with measurable benefits to their wellbeing. Many of the techniques they use involve connecting the thoughts of the brain and the emotions of the heart through different exercises. Some feel that this is the way into the soul, the way to reach that place where through our emotions we can combine our intentions with our actions to create authentic power for ourselves. By measuring these effects scientifically, studies have shown that actual changes take place in the genes, many of which are related to improvements in the functioning of the immune system.

Force of love

It was a revelation for me to discover how the soul 'connects' to the universal field of energy of which all living beings are a part. This discovery opened me up to receiving positive energy from people around me, which in turn promoted a spirit of healing. How do prayer, love and strong relationships promote and accelerate healing? In his observations of exceptional patients, Bernie Siegel gives huge credence to the importance of a strong support system and its positive impact on the healing and recovery of patients. In many religious traditions there are special prayers and different prayer groups that convene to pray for the sick and needy in their communities. This is what happened in my community and in other countries around the world where my family, friends and many people I did not even know came together to pray for my recovery. I was told about these prayer groups and could feel those energetic waves of love and concern reach into my soul during some of my darkest moments.

One of the most unusual experiences I had in relation to prayer and connection was when I was in in Tampa, Florida, for my CAR-T cell transplant. Tampa is not quite in the 'Bible Belt' of the southern states of America, yet I found most of the people that I interacted with – from hospital personnel to the Uber drivers to the checkout staff in the supermarket – were far more religiously connected than the average UK citizen. It wasn't just that people would utter 'God bless you' nonstop, it was their whole attitude to life. There was one particular driver who frequently collected me to go to the hospital and would always greet me with a story that reflected his deep beliefs such as 'I got up this morning and opened two gifts from God – my two eyes.' Another driver was full of jokes about God and Jesus. And there was one lovely, jolly, female Uber driver who, upon hearing why I was in Tampa, asked for my name, saying: 'I am going to put you in my prayers.' I was so moved by this gesture.

But the story doesn't end there. Members of my family had been taking it in turns to fly out to Tampa to be with me during my hospital stay, and three weeks after this encounter with the Uber driver, it was Tanya's turn. She ordered an Uber to drive her from the flat we had rented to the hospital, and upon hearing Tanya's English accent, the female driver asked Tanya where she was from and why was she in Tampa. Tanya explained that she had come to visit her mother who was in the hospital undergoing a new type of treatment for cancer. The driver replied: 'Oh I had a lady in my cab the other week, also from London, who had come for some special treatment.' My daughter replied, 'Oh that really is funny.' 'You know,' the driver continued, 'I even remember her name because I told her I was going to pray for her. Her name was Mindy.' 'That's so strange,' replied Tanya, 'because that's my mother. My mother is Mindy.' 'Well,' continued the driver in her wonderful southern drawl, 'Every day since I took Mindy in my taxi, I've been praying to the Lord for ma Mindy. Just this morning in the shower I was wondering how is ma Mindy, I wondered if she is getting any better and if I still needed to pray for her. And I asked God – You need to tell me if I still need to pray for ma Mindy. And then just before I picked you up, I had intended to go home but decided to do one more job and you came into my cab, and I hear from you that ma Mindy still needs ma prayers. I cannot believe this coincidence.'

Tanya told me afterwards that she came out of that cab shaking. When she came up to my hospital room and told me the story, I was lying in bed still very weak, but I nodded that I remembered that driver, and then I thought to myself, there is no such thing as coincidence. Whether you call it God working in mysterious ways or a sixth sense, either way that healing energy was sent to me even in Florida!

I have another personal story about the healing energy that can be transmitted through the soul, from many years back, when my parents were on holiday in Switzerland. My father suffered a sudden massive heart attack and tragically died there late Friday afternoon. When we received the fateful news in London, we realised that not one member of the family could fly out to be with my mother before Shabbat. We worried enormously about my mother and how she would cope being alone there until one of us could fly out after Shabbat, to help bring my father home. Although the owners of the Jewish hotel where she was staying were incredibly helpful and supportive, she didn't have anyone there that she knew. News of my father's sudden death spread rapidly around our community in London and over the next forty-eight hours, family and friends gathered around us, helping to share the burden of our grief, and thinking of my mother miles away all alone and what she was going through.

After my mother arrived back in London, accompanied by my husband and brother-in-law who had flown out after Shabbat to Switzerland, we asked her how on earth she coped during that very difficult time. She said that she didn't know how or where it came from, but she felt a force of strength enter her, which carried her through those fateful hours. In retrospect, knowing what I now know about the field of universal energy, I truly believe it was the love and sympathy of all of us who were thinking of her that initiated the creative dynamic of intentions of love and concern, which were transmitted to my mother, supporting her in her hour of need. My mother was always a loving and caring person throughout her life to those around her, and in her time of need the love was reciprocated. This is the law of karma in action.

If you stop and think about it, there are countless small incidents when invisible connections manifest themselves. How many times have you thought to call someone and at that very moment, they call you? Or you had intended to visit someone but bumped into them later that day? Some people refer to this as having a 'sixth sense', and I can attest that my mother-in-law was a perfect example of someone who was always in tune with other people, and could intuit their needs without them even having to express them.

Many people tell me that after all the challenges I have endured, I am an inspiration to them. I keep telling them that the courage I have to deal with both my illness and the death of my husband comes not just from trying to adopt a positive mindset, but also from the love and concern that people have given to me. Transmitted through the universal field of energy, this force of love has touched my soul and because I opened my heart to it, allowing it to penetrate my very being, I strongly believe that it has helped me to heal. I in turn could then convey that love and inspiration back to those around me. That is not to say that the forces of love and prayer that penetrate a sick or troubled person's soul can necessarily change the outcome of a person's recovery. Sometimes our souls have achieved what they needed to do in this physical realm, and it is time to pass on to the other side.

Since my husband's death, I have asked myself frequently why it is that after years of cancer treatment, I am still alive, while Johnny became ill and died within the space of two weeks. I have experienced great angst and guilt in trying to understand why this happened as my logical brain and my emotional heart pulled me in different directions. My thoughts were so intense that they fuelled my creativity in writing this book. At first, I attributed this surge of creativity to the therapeutic value of writing about my illness and bereavement. It took me many months to realise, though, that I was suffering from a syndrome called posttraumatic growth, something that I had never even heard of until I read about it in Sheryl Sandberg's *Option B*, a book she wrote after the sudden death of her husband at the age of forty-seven. I had gone through some deep soul-searching before Johnny's death, when I had my serious brushes with death during my cancer treatments. But Johnny's sudden passing caused such a huge disturbance in the very core of my being that it had awoken a part of my soul in a different way to how the trauma of my cancer diagnosis and treatments had affected me.

I suffered profoundly and questioned everything about who I was and what my life would be like without Johnny by my side, and that suffering and searching for answers led to a phenomenon called posttraumatic growth. Most people are familiar with the term posttraumatic stress, a state that many people suffer after experiencing trauma, but posttraumatic growth refers to a trauma that ends up being transformative, productive and positive for a person. It is through this growth that you learn to appreciate life more, living day to day with greater meaning. It is because your heart has not just been broken, but broken open through your trauma; it has opened so much that it has a greater capacity to hold within it not just the suffering, but joy and hope too. This 'brokenness' releases an energy that comes after internalising the trauma, which allows you to process the grief. By doing so, you don't hold on to the brokenness and retreat inwards, you allow yourself to open up to receive the emotions of love which heal you. Perhaps I had already started along this route during my illness and it just expanded after Johnny's death. That is difficult to judge looking back now, but one thing that definitely grew was the guilt I felt at undergoing a positive change following Johnny's death. I still can't explain why that happened, except to say that I am not sure this book would ever have been written had Johnny lived. But believe me, I would make that swap in a blink of an eye if I could.

In the fullness of time I have come to accept that the resilience I built came from listening to my soul, which told me that Johnny's time had come and his lifetime's purpose had been fulfilled. But this was not a passive surrender – it was a deep and fearless acceptance of the present moment of life as it is now. I had to accept this as truth in order to move forward with my life.

Connecting to that inner voice

So much of what is understood now as heart wisdom comes from the wisdom of traditional beliefs, religions and habits of the ancient world. It is from these sources that we understand the purpose of the soul and the wisdom that guides our lives. As the world moved forward after the industrial revolution, followed by the huge scientific advances of the past two centuries, much of this wisdom was lost or seen as irrelevant in a culture that was becoming increasingly secular and distant from faith and spirituality.

Ironically, in today's post-religious world, spirituality (especially in the West) is being rediscovered not through religion but through practices such as meditation, yoga, tai chi and other martial arts. Whereas fifty years ago these practices were marginalised for deriving from Eastern cultures and religions, they have now become mainstream in Western societies where people are looking for relief from lifestyles that leave them ever more stressed.

As Rabbi Steinsaltz says about our way of life in today's world with its ongoing stimuli: '[It] takes both time and attention and does not leave room for many internally focused thoughts. Consequentially while our external reality grows more extensive, more fast-paced and more demanding, our internal reality is constantly shrinking.' But if you can create an intention to deliberately silence the noises of life, and listen instead to that inner voice, you will be able to connect with your soul. And this is where meditation comes to the fore.

I came to meditation through yoga, which I began practising twenty years ago. I had been suffering for many years with joint issues and found that yoga exercises helped my body to relax and stretch out in ways that could make moving easier and less painful. During the classes I learnt about the chukras and the flow of energy around the body, and about how to deal with stress in life, by lifting the blockages in those chukras. Each ninety-minute lesson would end with half an hour of breathing, relaxation and meditation. But as I said earlier, yoga at that point was just a small part of my life and not intrinsic to the way I lived.

In recent years I have reconnected with the practice of meditation and it is now part of my daily routine, as I understood that it is one the foremost techniques that can have a real positive effect on the body. The world of meditation and energy healing has developed enormously in recent years with techniques including visualisation and energy freedom techniques (tapping), a variety of martial arts including yoga, tai chi and qigong, reiki healing, and many other techniques of releasing energy blockages in the body, which allows freedom of movement for the energy in the body physically, mentally and spiritually.

Whatever challenge you're facing, I strongly recommend taking up meditation. It can, however, be overwhelming, when trying to incorporate meditation into your daily life, to sift through the different meditation techniques in books, videos and social media. I have recommended two books on meditation in the bibliography at the end, but each person has to discover what works for them. Some of the visualisations I use in meditation have come from Dr Dispenza's books and videos and others I found after searching on YouTube.

The practice of meditation focuses on the breath and there are many breathing exercises that connect us to our inner being, our soul. I have been thinking about meditation and how it connects with our inner world in such a profound way. The Hebrew word for 'to breathe' is *linshom*, the root of which is the three Hebrew letters *nun*, *shin* and *mem*. One of the Hebrew words for soul is *neshamah*, which has the same root letters – *nun*, *shin* and *mem*. I believe that, like many words that have the same root letters in Hebrew, this is not coincidental. The way we connect to our souls is through our breath, for without breathing the physical body cannot exist. This is the bridge between our physical self and our spiritual self. When God created the first human, He 'breathed the breath of life' into man's body so that he became a living being.

Deep intentional breathing helps us to focus on our inner

world. If we can silence all the noise in our life and concentrate our thoughts inwards, it can help us listen to our souls. Meditation is one of the best ways to raise your body's energy to a higher frequency, boosting your immune system, by connecting your heart and your brain. And this penetrates into your soul.

It has not always been easy for me to connect to that inner voice. At times when I was overwhelmed by the challenges in my life, it was hard to still all those outside noises and turn my mind inwards. But I kept trying and I have succeeded on so many occasions to listen to the wisdom of my soul by opening up to the emotions of my heart.

Stepping

Lessons I have learnt about the wisdom of the soul and the emotions of the heart

- Soul-searching often occurs when faced with an external challenge that disturbs the normal pattern of your life.

- Your soul is the seat of your inner wisdom and direction, and the positive energy it creates by the intentions you give to your actions can be your force for change.

- The connections between your soul and other souls can come through thoughts or prayers.

- Invisible connections will manifest themselves, so be ready to enjoy the magic of their appearance in your lives.

- Tuning in to your inner wisdom can come about through methods, such as meditation, that silence the outside noises in your life.

Pathway Six
Cultivating Gratitude – Counting Your Blessings

'Gratitude is not only the greatest of virtues, but the parent of all others.'
— CICERO

DIARY ENTRY: *July 2018*

'Flip out' – no I haven't lost it…that's the name of the local trampoline place which has become a favourite indoor venue with children, and the place I recently took my two granddaughters, Noa and Libbie, for an afternoon's entertainment, as they had come to London for a visit from Israel. It struck me as I watched the two of them performing somersaults, jumping up and down and landing in a pit of cushioning foam, that bringing them to this place was a metaphor for so much of what I have been through in recent years. As my life alternated between the high and low points of illness and bereavement, I have been so blessed that when I fell, I was cushioned by the love of my family and friends.

That afternoon was fun, quality time as I watched them perform so much of what they have learnt in their years of gymnastic classes. I have learnt to treasure these moments which have become so important because they have been so infrequent. My trips to Israel to see them have depended on my treatment schedule, and have been few and far between, and their trips to London even less frequent. So, as I said, treasured moments when I count my blessings.

I realised that what has kept me going through the ups and downs I have experienced has been precisely this, to have been able to watch them grow and develop into the wonderful children and soon-to-be teenagers that they are. Even more so, since Johnny passed away, I feel a very deep desire and responsibility to keep going, to still be around not just for my children and grandchildren but for all the wider family. And it is they who have cushioned me in love, and moments like these touch me deeply with a sense of gratitude for all that I am blessed with.

Hopefully I won't be 'flipping out' any time soon. I will be keeping things going through the ups and downs that have somersaulted through my life, landing wherever possible within the pillars of support of my wonderful family and friends, for which I am eternally grateful.

Giving and receiving

One of the hardest adjustments, in the early years of my cancer journey, was shifting from a mode of giving to that of receiving. Many people are 'givers' in different ways. They give their time, energy and resourcefulness to helping others, whether to their immediate or wider family, or generally those in need. I cannot say that I was forever busy with the above, but at certain moments giving did occupy a significant amount of my time and gave me a sense of purpose and satisfaction.

It was therefore a major change for me to suddenly become a recipient of so many acts of kindness and thoughtfulness. Once people knew about my situation when I started having treatment, the kindness just kept on flowing. *Chessed* in its deepest sense. It came not just from close family and friends, but often from people with whom I did not have regular interaction. Some of the messages, phone calls and food deliveries I received brought me to tears. It was truly humbling and very overwhelming. It actually got to a point where it became too difficult to internalise. It was then that I undertook many months of counselling to help me cope with my new situation. I needed to be able to open up my heart to the amount of love, concern and thoughtfulness that was coming my way from those around me. I had to understand that I had given so much in the past to my family and those around me and now it was my time to be on the receiving end. I needed help to shift to a mindset that could accept and internalise this new reality. I opened myself up to receiving love, positivity and warmth – and treasured those positive emotions so deeply that I felt the experience was healing.

It's not that this was the first time I felt appreciated in my life. My children often wrote me thank you notes at certain significant moments in their lives. Others have written to thank our family and offer their appreciation for a variety of reasons. So it is not that acts of kindness have gone unnoticed or unremarked. But when one is struck with the misfortune of a serious illness or a sudden bereavement, life is no longer taken for granted, and appreciation for every small thing becomes a part of your life. It made me realise that really there are only three major things that make life worth living: your health, a roof over your head with daily sustenance, and the love and support of family and friends. Everything else is just a bonus and if you are lucky enough to be blessed with those things, you must be grateful for every minute of it.

Giving and receiving. Throughout our lives, we do both of these things. I always thought that I got so much more out of being able to give rather than receive, and I think this was what made it so hard for me to stop giving, and be on the passive end of receiving. Once my treatment began, I was no longer in the position to be able to give to people in the same way I had done in the past. I likened my situation to the transmission of an electrical signal. You have a transmitter that gives out the signal, but unless you have a receiver which can accept and process that signal, then the circuit is not complete and the transmission of the electrical current won't work. So it is with human interaction. There are givers and receivers and I realised that at different times in life, under different circumstances, we move between the two. What I have also come to understand throughout the years is that friends and family need to feel useful. In allowing them to give, and then receiving their help with grace and appreciation, you are completing the circuit. You are allowing the energy to flow from them to you. And it is this energy that helps you to heal.

Gratitude rather than thanks

Gratitude is not quite the same as giving thanks. From an early age we are taught to thank people for their kindnesses. 'Say thank you to grandma for the lovely present she bought you.' 'Don't forget to thank your teacher for helping you out with your project.' 'You must thank the gentleman for finding your dolly that you dropped in the street,' and so on. As children we are taught to say brachot to thank God every day for everything He has done for us.

Giving thanks to show one's appreciation is a positive action, but gratitude is an emotion. It is something more profound that comes when giving thanks has been taken from its external manifestation and internalised and processed. Gratitude is a feeling that touches the heart in response to being the beneficiary of a gift of some kind, which is often felt to be undeserved by the receiver. Gratitude is what I experienced as I explained earlier when I discussed the concept of *chessed*. The gratitude I felt to those around me who supported me with even small gestures was profound and internalised, even though I didn't feel I had done anything to deserve their kindnesses. In so many instances I felt that they had gone above and beyond as there was no way at the time I could reciprocate.

Gratitude is also felt in a metaphysical way towards a higher power, an external connection where you acknowledge the goodness of your life. This is what I felt and still feel when I count my blessings every day, and even in the most difficult of circumstances

I try to find something for which to be grateful. Yet there are people who are at such a low point in their lives that they may feel there is nothing to be grateful for. Trying to change your attitude when you feel broken inside is the most difficult thing of all. Nonetheless, if you try to connect to something outside of yourself, even one small thing can provide a ray of hope or light that will begin your journey to living in grace.

Sometimes the gratitude you experience can be a combination of both human interaction and grace from a higher power. This is what I felt at different times during my cancer journey, when I had cause to be grateful for the expertise of the medical teams and the love and concern of my family and friends and at the same time be in awe of the higher power that carried me through my recovery. One powerful example of this type of gratitude was when I was at the Moffitt Cancer Centre in Tampa and had just completed my three-week inpatient stay after my CAR-T cell treatment. The time had come for my discharge and the hospital staff who had looked after me all gathered in the corridor outside my room beside a large brass bell. It was a custom in the hospital that each patient, on completion of their treatment, when they were well enough to leave, would ring the bell announcing their recovery. This was to give hope to other patients, who upon hearing the bell ring, would be uplifted and feel that they too could recover soon.

I was still quite weak but managed to get out of my wheelchair and I rang that bell with all the strength I could muster. As the sound of it reverberated through the corridor, the staff all clapped and cheered; I felt lifted up in a way that is hard to describe. The sound of chiming bells is a sound associated with both joyous occasions and sad commemorations, and that day for me was both. It was joyous because of the deep gratitude I felt, thanking God for being able to have accessed this lifesaving new treatment, and to have had my children and members of my family taking it in turns to be with me throughout my stay. They had each travelled thousands of miles across the world to Tampa to make sure I was not left alone for one minute while I was there. But it was sad too because I no longer had Johnny by my side to see how far I had come. Yet despite the bittersweet nature of this moment, the gratitude I felt as I rang that bell was powerful: gratitude for all the forces that had come together to enable me to reach that point in my journey. I counted my blessings and I continue to do so every single day.

Counting those blessings connects us to those around us, and to God. Feeling gratitude acknowledges those relationships and validates both our worth and the worth of those who are involved in our lives.

I have experienced so much gratitude during recent years and there is no doubt that it has deepened my appreciation for so many things in my life, and facilitated my healing by helping me come to a deeper realisation of what really counts in life, and how much I have been blessed with. But like all emotions, you have to open yourself up to it; you have to be in the right mental state to accept blessings. Cultivating gratitude moves you into a state of graciousness, which in the long run helps bring you to a state of peace with yourself and those around you. All of this will help you to heal.

Gratitude and healing

That gratitude can cause healing is not anecdotal. It has been proven through various scientific studies, including diary-keeping, where two groups were asked to note positive and negative events. Brain activity was measured using magnetic resonance. The results showed that those who practised gratitude each day were more optimistic and positive about their lives, more physically active and reported fewer visits to a doctor than those that only recorded negative events. Their findings suggest that gratitude stimulates the hypothalamus to secrete hormones that have a beneficial effect on the physical healing of the body.

In recent years I have often asked myself if surviving a life-threatening illness has made me a better person. Has being appreciated made me a better person? I don't think I am easily able to answer those questions. But what I can say is that my experience has made me a more grateful person, appreciative of each little blessing that comes my way, be it a glorious sunset, an unexpected visitor, or just a FaceTime session with my grandchildren. I have become better at managing my priorities and cultivating gratitude within myself, which has helped me appreciate the blessings in my life.

There is a wonderful story I once heard about how being grateful for things, even before you actually possess them, can generate faith and positivity and bring healing. In a certain Indian tribal area, there had been no rain for many months and the crops were failing, so they began to perform rain dances and recite prayers asking the heavens to open and send rain. But there was one boy who didn't take part. Instead he took himself off to the fields and started to dig ditches. The elders admonished him, asking why he was digging ditches when the rain hadn't yet come. He replied: 'The rain will come and I am giving thanks for it in advance by preparing for it.' He would not accept the lack of rain; he was demonstrating gratitude for the rain falling by digging the ditches in preparation, fully anticipating that it would come. Sure enough, once he completed the ditches the rain started to fall.

Much of what I have written in the preceding pathways about creating thoughts that can change body chemistry is related to envisioning a future where you have the things that you currently do not possess; envisioning a time when there is no deficiency in your life; where you are happy with what you have. By practising gratitude, you are saying just that: I am happy with what I have or what I hope I will have. I have visualised so many times being well, being with my family, as well as many more dreams of what I want to achieve in the future. This approach has helped me not just survive, but thrive.

But being grateful while dealing with an illness is one thing. Finding gratitude while enduring a bereavement is quite another. Even though gratitude is the ultimate in receiving, and has the power to heal, it is extremely difficult while mourning the loss of someone you love to find any redeeming features that allow you to open your heart to receive. However, you have to try, for although there is no gratitude in the trauma of death itself, gratitude can be found in giving thanks for having had that person in your life, for what they have meant to you over the years, and I am immensely grateful for the forty wonderful years that Johnny and I shared bringing up our family. Yet I now try to appreciate aspects of my life alone as I go forward without Johnny by my side. I am extremely fortunate to have wonderful children who together with my two sisters and all their families have supported and cared for me throughout. Our relationships were always strong but dealing with the challenges since Johnny passed away has brought us even closer. I also have a wonderful circle of friends who have been there for me throughout the years. I have tried to enjoy the new sense of independence, where I am no longer answerable or accountable to anyone for how I spend my time. Although I miss Johnny, and there is no denying that there are many moments of loneliness, I am lucky in that I do not feel alone and in reality am always surrounded by family and friends. I am also lucky to be one of those people who enjoys their own company, and for this I am extremely grateful. Although writing this book has not been easy, it has been extremely therapeutic for me and I am grateful that I have the ability to express my feelings in such a creative way.

Being appreciated and appreciative

Many years ago, while we were sitting shivah for our father, an elderly gentleman that none of us recognised, came in and sat with us. He proceeded to tell us how our father was a tzaddik[1] who helped him start off in business many years ago, giving him goods with open credit. This was not an isolated story. As the shivah continued, friends and family recounted many stories of how our father had supported and helped people in many different ways – so many wonderful aspects of my father that we didn't know or fully appreciate while he was alive. Why did it take his death for

---

1. Righteous person.

us to be aware? Wouldn't it be wonderful to be appreciated during your lifetime?

Some of the emails, letters and texts our family received after Johnny died were not only wonderfully comforting, but also detailed with great fondness the various ways Johnny had affected people's lives. Over the years I had lost contact with some of the people who wrote to us, yet they recalled with immense gratitude how Johnny had helped them and reached out to them. He was remembered as a young teenager welcoming an 'out of the crowd' person into the centre of the *chevrah*,[2] as well as later on in life helping a person through the rituals of mourning. These small acts of kindness had not been forgotten, and I am sure Johnny would have been grateful for their appreciation. But even though he isn't here to hear this outpouring of love and appreciation, we are – and these memories mean an enormous amount to all our family. My son-in-law Ian collected every single one of these messages into a huge file, which is now a constant reminder to us of what Johnny's life meant to so many people.

I am inordinately grateful that I have been shown appreciation during my lifetime. It's not that I sought it out but it has demonstrated the kindness and gratefulness of others, and in turn I have had the opportunity to thank others for their kindnesses, especially in recent years. But it makes me sad now to look back and think that my father died before I had time to tell him how truly grateful I was to him for not only giving me life, but for everything that he did for us over the years, providing for us and creating a safe and happy environment in which my sisters and I could flourish.

My mother was one of the most grateful and gracious people I know. She was a deeply religious woman, not in the sense that she spent all day praying, but rather in her connection to God. Not a day went by without her expressing her gratitude to Him for the blessings He had bestowed on her. Although, like me, she lost her husband suddenly when she was only in her mid-sixties, she

---

2. Social circle.

never complained and was forever grateful for the family she had been blessed with. She had a kind, caring and quiet nature and was continually optimistic, no matter what happened. And at only 4ft 11in tall, we used to say that her heart was so big it was completely out of proportion to her stature. Even my father, who towered a foot over her, would remark that he looked up to her. One of my enduring memories of her was on Friday night as she lit candles when she brought in Shabbat. She would bring a chair next to the candles and sit there for almost half an hour with her eyes covered just talking to God and thanking him for each and every member of her family. Such was her gratitude for life's blessings.

Having arrived in the UK as a refugee, my mother was lucky in that her whole family managed to escape from Germany before World War II. She had lost her former comfortable life in Berlin and had to start over again in a strange country, but she never dwelt on her losses; she and her family built anew and were grateful to be alive, positive about their future. I learnt so much from my mother not by what she told me to do, but from how she acted and conducted herself. As Rabbi Abraham Joshua Heschel once wrote, there are textbooks that teach us lessons and there are text people who are living lessons from whom we can learn so much. And my mother was a living lesson in gratitude.

I had another blessing that I never took for granted, and that was my relationship with my in-laws, Johnny's parents Zoli and Gerda, who were the warmest and kindest people. They were, in truth, a second set of parents to me. My mother-in-law Gerda, like my mother, arrived in the UK on the Kindertransport before the war broke out. She came from an extremely privileged background in Hamburg, yet she left it all behind when her mother sent her and her two sisters to the safety of England, where her father had escaped to after being arrested in Germany. She waved goodbye to her mother at the railway platform at the age of seventeen, never to see her again, because she perished in Auschwitz. Like so many survivors and refugees who lost so much, Gerda had every reason to be bitter at life, to keep looking back with sadness, but instead she chose to live life with positivity and gratitude. I know that she missed her mother, but she never missed any of the physical trappings of wealth that surrounded her in her youth. She had a hard life here and it took many years for her and my father-in-law, also a refugee, to build a comfortable life for their family, but she never complained. She had a wonderful warmth and generosity of spirit that made her the focus of her family and friends and I was welcomed into their home with open arms as their own daughter. Not everyone is lucky in life with their in-laws, but I am so grateful for I know I was blessed to win the lottery.

Just as gratitude is an emotion of love, so is joy. In fact, gratitude produces joy. And as is often the theme in many of the pathways in this book, you need to work on yourself in order to arrive at healing. For any type of healing to materialise, or indeed any form of progression in your life, you need to be an active participant. Gratitude is no exception. Cultivating, finding, coping, awakening, forgiving, rekindling – the headings I used for the healing pathways in this book are verbs because we must actively seek our own healing. In order to heal you need to actively create a new reality for yourself.

Stepping Stones

Lessons I have learnt about cultivating gratitude and counting my blessings

- We give and receive at different times in our lives and it is important to understand that this completes a circuit through which energy flows.

- When on the receiving end, open yourself up to accept from those giving you help, for this will move you into a state of grace and help your healing.

- Gratitude can be felt from internalising the interactions with other people or from acknowledgement of the Divine presence in your life.

- See the blessing in these interactions for through this you recognise the worth of yourself and others in the relationship.

- Being grateful for what you have in the present moment means you are acknowledging your blessings.

Pathway Seven
Rekindling Joy –
Awakening to Awe

'Find out where joy resides, and give it a voice far beyond singing. For to miss the joy is to miss all.'

— ROBERT LOUIS STEVENSON

DIARY ENTRY: *November 2017*

'All the leaves are brown and the sky is grey...'

At this time of year, the Mamas and Papas song reverberates in my head as I look out the window watching the rain pour down from a dark, cloudy sky. Yet autumn is a wonderful time of year, despite the fact that it is a harbinger of winter's long dark nights and cold grey days. The profusion of colours and bracing changeable weather makes it one of the most interesting seasons. As I look back over the past year since my transplant it is easy to believe that I lost months of my life, as I do not remember much about last autumn or winter; so many of my days were spent lying in a hospital bed, not part of a world that turned without me.

Taking a walk in my local park recently reminded me that I am very much alive and part of this world. The beauty of autumn colours, the crisp air, the rustling leaves and the bustling of people stirred my spirit and screamed at me:

'There is no such thing as losing time, only time passing during which things happen of which we are not always aware.' During those long days without end, my body was fighting for survival and for a few brief months earlier this year we really thought it was winning. But as we all know, we are not always masters of our fate or captains of our destiny. These past few months have been filled with yet further treatments, hospitalisation and more flights for our incredible children who have supported us from afar and constantly travelled to be with us during these difficult times. Nevertheless, the capacity that remains within me to enjoy simple moments of beauty in nature keeps my spirit intact and ready to face whatever comes next.

Living in the shadow of a serious illness meant that I developed and cultivated a deeper sense of meaning in my life and this led me to live with a sense of awe at the everyday aspects of life. When I was younger, and had less time to think, as a busy mother, daughter, student, and professional, life just seemed to flow from day to day. There were fleeting moments, though, when I experienced a sense of awe that raised me from my everyday existence. At that time, I did not understand the significance or the wider implications of this transcendence.

The first time I sat in a concert hall as a teenager listening to a Beethoven symphony, I started to cry at the sheer beauty of the music. The first time I set eyes on a Van Gogh painting, the colours hit me with a such a visceral force that I was instantly hooked on Impressionism, and have loved all the artists from that period ever since. I did not realise that the profound emotion I was experiencing on those occasions was transcendence in its purest form, a lifting of my soul to connect with something above and beyond the mundane. At other times, being in places of immense beauty or sharing joyous moments with family and friends created deep emotional experiences, which I now appreciate have contributed to the sheer joy of being alive. And joy is very much a transformative emotion. It is the emotion of awakening to the transcendental experience of awe.

When times are difficult, when it is an effort just to get up each day and face the world, it can feel almost impossible to summon joy. But it is the rekindling of joy that can help to heal you, for joy is so much more than just happiness. In David Brooks' book, *The Second Mountain,* he writes: 'Joy is a fuller richer state beyond happiness ... it involves a loss of self as you feel fused to something other than yourself... While happiness is an expansion of self... and tends to be fickle and fleeting, joy can be fundamental and enduring.' Happiness is a state of being related to an external experience, but joy is internal and connected spiritually to the soul. Yet, in many ways it is even more than this. Joy is not dependent on timing or being sought after. It can appear at any time in any place. It doesn't require any validation from any source; it is intrinsic in itself to the person experiencing it and there are so many things that can trigger the emotion. And that emotion does not deny the reality of the present, it just puts it into perspective.

But how can you bring joy back into your life when your body and heart are broken; when you are living with fear and anger, pain and suffering? The truth is that it's not easy and anyone who thinks that one morning you will just wake up and see the light, both literally and metaphorically, is speaking about the very rare exceptions and not the majority of people in this situation. It takes time and an understanding of the phrase 'this too shall pass'. Hopefully each day your pain lessens and you start to heal. The steps can be incremental, but each small one will slowly help pull you out of the depths of despair.

Finding solace

One mitigating factor can be seeking solace, finding a way to assuage your suffering. For many, this also involves an awakening to awe, an awakening to the beauty around us. It can be something as simple as enjoying the stillness of a woodland, listening to a piece of sublime music, reading a book that touches you, looking at a beautiful painting, or just witnessing a magnificent sunset. Awakening yourself to the beauty around you can give you a feeling of connectedness to something bigger than yourself, and can create joy, even if it is not enduring. Every experience has the power not only to bring solace, but to transport you to another realm and can certainly be a healing force for a troubled and grieving soul. Every person will find comfort in something different, but as with so many aspects of our lives, we need to be open to the experience. We need to appreciate how it touches us and the benefit it brings us. For joy has the power to transform suffering.

Taking walks in natural surroundings has always filled me with joy and wonder. I have never lost the ability to marvel at the changing seasons, from the bare tree branches in winter to the buds of spring and the profusion of different shades of green on the leaves in the summer. And as I wrote in my diary entry, autumn has its own incredible colourful array. Walking in the mountains or along a coastal path have been some of my favourite destinations. It is often time spent with nature that gives us moments of transcendence, where we find a sense of meaning in our lives that is beyond ourselves. Johnny and I spent many happy summer holidays walking in the splendour of the Italian Dolomites and the Swiss Alps, and my childhood is full of wonderful memories of seaside holidays. In fact, the sea has been a source of great solace to me over the years. There is something that resonates so deeply with my soul as I watch the waves break with their plumes of foam on the sand and then wash back into the ocean. The vastness of blue water brings many people a feeling of peace and tranquillity. The sea was something that brought enormous comfort to me after Johnny died. There is something so life-affirming about being by the sea. I am not sure if it is the immensity of the body of water or just the physical motion of watching the waves. I stayed in Netanya for the week after Johnny's *shivah*, and as I watched the Mediterranean stretching out in front of me with the sky's expanse above, I deeply felt Johnny's presence. There was a feeling of transcendence; it wasn't just Johnny with me, but also God. My whole family gathered together and we fortified each other with the knowledge that Johnny is watching over us and that we will get through whatever lies ahead.

Rabbi Abraham Joshua Heschel wrote: 'Our goal should be to live life in radical amazement…get up in the morning and look at the world in a way that takes nothing for granted. Everything is phenomenal; everything is incredible, never treat life casually. To be spiritual is to be amazed.' Of course, we cannot go around all day in a state of rapture, for it would be impossible to live like that, and not everyone has the spiritual capacity to see life that way. But there should be moments when we are truly present, noticing our surroundings and consequently feeling grateful for what we have. We should stop and count our blessings and with this should come the joy of what it is to appreciate life in its fullest sense.

The healing power of laughter

One of the beautiful aspects of the relationship that Johnny and I shared over the years was the capacity he had to make me laugh, which in a way brought me not just happiness but that deeper sense of joy. For laughter is one of the basic expressions of happiness, joy and love, curing a multitude of ills and is often quoted as being the best medicine. Laughter has always played an important role in my life, as it did for Johnny too. It was actually one of the reasons I married him – he made me laugh, and a girl can never resist a happy, funny man. Throughout our forty-year marriage, Johnny's sense of humour kept me going through some difficult times and so many happy times too, and it was these memories that help nourish me when he is no longer physically by my side.

Laughter can mitigate the effects of stress in the body. It can alter dopamine and serotonin activity and increase endorphins, which helps people improve their mood and there is no doubt that laughter can help heal people in so many different situations. Laughter therapy is now recognised as an effective mechanism aiding the recovery of many patients and has been adopted by hospitals and clinics. Medical clowns began entertaining patients in the 1970s, with the setting up of the Gesundheit Institute by Hunter

Doherty 'Patch' Adams, a doctor portrayed so vividly by the actor Robin Williams in the film *Patch Adams*. Today medical clowns can be found in many hospitals, and especially children's centres.

One of the healthiest responses to life is laughter. Apart from reducing stress, boosting your immunity and combating depression, laughter can lessen pain and increase your resilience. It is also contagious. The discovery of mirror neurons, the nerve cells that cause us to mirror the behaviour we witness in others, is the reason why we smile when someone smiles at us. A sense of humour is an important trait that is high on the list of priorities when looking for a partner as our bodies like the feeling of shared laughter which fosters a closeness and a deep sense of wellbeing.

As is carved on his gravestone, and written in the dedication to this book, Johnny was a man who brought love and laughter into my life. But not just mine, he brought it to everyone who crossed his path in life, whether socially or in business, despite the fact that he was actually quite a shy person. During his *shivah*, which was a sad and difficult time, one of the most surprising sounds often heard in the room was laughter. It came as our family and friends spent hours talking about so many aspects of Johnny's life that had touched them. People remembered with great fondness and amusement the hours they spent in Johnny's company and the things he would get up to. In this way, the *shivah* is part of the healing process. For a whole week we were constantly surrounded by family and friends, being forced out of ourselves, when the natural inclination during bereavement is to retreat within yourself and hide away from the world. Talking and reminiscing about Johnny in the company of others helped to restore a meaning to his life and ours. The rabbis that instituted the mourning rituals of Judaism certainly understood the therapeutic value of it. For in the depth of great sorrow, one can still rekindle the memories of joy.

And rekindling joy through laughter is more than a coping mechanism, it is also a healing mechanism for the body. As I talked about earlier, so many positive chemical reactions are triggered in the body by the action of laughter and the emotion of happiness and joy that it elicits. Throughout my challenges in life, I have always tried to preserve my sense of humour. Jews, who are no strangers to suffering, are known for their sense of humour, even when sometimes it is filled with deep irony. In fact, some of the best Jewish comedians, authors and filmmakers have created a reality that portrays the absurdities of life with humour.

Rabbi Sacks discusses this concept in relation to the Jewish festival of Purim. He writes about the therapeutic nature of joy, something which I have discussed within the healing framework of the individual, but he places it within a national perspective. 'The Jewish response to trauma is counterintuitive and extraordinary. You defeat fear by joy. You conquer terror by collective celebration...You are declaring you will not be intimidated and you surround yourself with the single most effective antidote to fear; joy in life itself.'

Beauty in the ordinary

Laughter, humour and trying to see the positive in difficult situations have helped me keep a sense of perspective as I have worked through dealing with everything from cancer treatment to bereavement. Thinking back to the memories I have of Johnny, his lust for life and his great sense of humour, captured in countless videos and photographs over the years, have helped to rekindle joy in me, even though it is tinged with a sense of sadness that I no longer have him by my side. Johnny had an amazing ability to retain not only his boyish charm, but his sense of wonder, which in a way is a part of childhood. Possessing a sense of awe in viewing everyday experiences with wonder is something that seems to get lost as childhood passes and you become more discerning, and in many ways, discriminating adults. Yes, we can experience awe seeing an incredible landscape for the first time, witnessing the birth of a child or sharing a special joyous celebration, but we should equally be able to look around at our everyday surroundings and, as Heschel says, take nothing for granted.

Much of what brings us joy and solace is related to love and finding meaning in our lives. The experience of transcendence, which is often sudden and fleeting, can be given permanence through a deeper understanding of finding a purpose in our lives. In so many ways, rediscovering awe and rekindling joy can help you cope and overcome challenges. And it isn't until you are dealing with a crisis that you reach that understanding.

When I was lying in the intensive care unit after I suffered serious life-threatening complications from my stem cell transplant, I tried to focus on what I had to live for; what gave my life meaning and purpose. I knew that I had to get better; I knew that I wanted to stay alive to be with my family and to see my grandchildren growing up. It was the love of my family and friends that sustained me and gave meaning to all that I had. It was time spent with them that brought the greatest joy into my life. This, in addition to the need I felt to fulfil so many more of the things I had planned to do, was what kept me going. I knew that I had to fight my fears and focus instead on visualising all my plans for the future. These positive thoughts have helped me immeasurably during so many difficult times over the years. Fixing my gaze on the light at the end of the tunnel helped to give me courage to continue through challenging times.

There are examples of many Holocaust survivors who managed to move forward with their lives by searching for meaning and holding on to that small spark that brought them hope and joy. Viktor Frankl, the world-famous psychiatrist, developed a whole new school of psychotherapy called 'logotherapy' based on his experiences in Auschwitz. He found that those inmates who had 'what to live for' fared better than those who had lost hope. As Nietzsche famously stated: 'He who has a why to live can bear almost any how.' Having a reason to continue in life and holding on to those things that are precious aren't just coping strategies but actually are the source of solace and comfort. Frankl expands this idea further by defining self-transcendence, a state that can be achieved not by looking for self-actualisation, but rather by focusing outwards, beyond the self, to something larger. He recounts an incident when he and his fellow prisoners were walking from one concentration camp to another. Suddenly they were awestruck by the beauty of watching a sunset. How incredible that in the direst of human circumstances man still has the capacity for awe, the capacity to transcend his current circumstances.

I came across a great book, *Lighter We Go*, by another Mindy – Mindy Greenstein – who is a clinical psychologist. She wrote the book with her mother, Jimmie Holland, about ageing. She writes: 'Transcendence can come from something as small as a cup of cocoa or as large as an act of emotional survival, as immediate as a moment in time or as long lasting as a general attitude toward life.' And it is your attitude to life that is so critical, and the underpinning of every pathway that helps you to heal. An attitude that allows you to open your heart to recognising with awe that which is around you, but that you have been disconnected from, will help you to rekindle joy.

There is a beautiful paragraph I read in Jeff Foster's book, *Falling in Love With Where You Are,* that illustrates how a change in attitude can influence how you interpret any given situation: 'Life will eventually bring you to your knees. Either you'll be on your knees cursing the universe and begging for a different life, or you'll be brought to your knees by gratitude and awe, deeply embracing the life you have, too overwhelmed by the beauty of it all to stand or even to speak. Either way they are the same knees.'

Rubin's Vase

Old Woman and Young Girl

Take a look at Rubin's Vase. Depending on how you look at it, it can also be seen as the side profiles of two faces. The second image can also be seen in two ways, either as a young girl or an old woman. It is how we choose to perceive what we are seeing and experiencing that determines our reactions. Even the word 'awe' has two distinct meanings. In the terminology in which I have used it in this pathway it is interpreted as wonder and amazement, yet the other meaning of awe is fear and dread. Two opposite meanings of one word, known as a contronym, so aptly describes what I mentioned about the two distinct emotions, love and fear, that govern all emotions. Awe as wonder is love; awe as dread is fear. This is perhaps what Jeff Foster was referring to in the quote above. We are where we are, and we can either see it as a blessing or a curse. The attitude we adopt to the situation we find ourselves in creates our world view.

During some of my darkest times, I wasn't sure if I would ever be able to experience that deep sense of joy again. In the midst of what I referred to earlier as the 'dark night of the soul', many people feel this way. Yet I tried to wake each day and count my blessings and force myself to realise that they outweighed any curse that had been inflicted upon me. Yes, I was being treated for cancer, but I was also surrounded by loving and supportive family and friends and they were carrying me through it all. When Johnny died, it was they who were the pillars that supported me and my children, and the glue that held us all together. I opened my heart to these blessings and I was, and still am, grateful for each and every one of them and this has allowed me to rekindle joy in my life and awaken to the ongoing awe of being truly alive in this world.

Stepping  Stones

Lessons I have learnt about rekindling joy and awakening to awe

- The attitude with which we view our experiences will determine how we react to them.
- The deep nature of joy is when happiness is internalised and touches your soul by fusing it to something outside of itself.
- In difficult times, seeking solace through finding a connection to nature can help revive a troubled spirit.
- Transcendence can come from experiencing something small or large and it helps you to cultivate awe in your life and enables you to count your blessings.
- Humour and laughter help to create an atmosphere where the burdens of life can be lifted.
- Finding meaning in your life helps you connect to that deeper sense of transcendence.

Pathway Eight

Forgiveness is a Gift – Letting Go a Release

'There is a huge freedom that comes to you when you take nothing personally.'

— DON MIGUEL RUIZ

DIARY ENTRY: *August 2020*

When I was looking through my diary entries to find a suitable one to fit this pathway on forgiveness, I realised that I didn't have one. I didn't want to make one up so I thought I would actually write a new one about the times in the past when I had to practise forgiveness. There is always one person in a relationship who has to be more forgiving, who is the one who gives in more often in order to preserve the peace; and in my marriage that person was me. Johnny was an amazing person, but not a very forgiving one. We all want to look back with rose-tinted spectacles and believe everything in the past was perfect, but that is not always the case. Don't get me wrong, he was an incredible loving husband, father and son, but he was not a person who easily tolerated anyone who crossed him or didn't agree with his points of view. He was a man who would always stick to his principles, upholding the values he held dear. So in order to keep the peace, it would usually be me who gave in. But even though these occasions were very infrequent, they left me feeling angry and upset, and I have come to realise that holding on to those emotions kept me in a kind of stranglehold. Eventually, my pent-up emotions would dissipate within a few days and things would return to normal. I needed to forgive him and just take it as part and parcel of family relationships, for over the years I learnt to understand where he was coming from and he began to understand my points of view. Yet when I became ill that whole argumentative side of him seemed to subside; perhaps he saw that forgiveness was something that he needed to do for himself as well as for others.

Think about the verb 'forgive'. What does it mean to you? The dictionary provides a few definitions: to stop feeling anger and resentment towards a person or at an accusation that caused upset or harm; to pardon; to be free from a debt.

Many people interpret forgiveness to mean 'giving in', or 'relinquishing blame'. It can be difficult to forgive someone if you still feel hurt or angry. However, even though forgiveness is not an easy thing to practise, it is an essential prerequisite for any form of healing. When you forgive, you free yourself from the people and situations that caused you suffering. Letting go of the anger and fear that you experienced from having been betrayed is not the same as giving in. You're not letting the person who hurt you off the hook. It is not a defeat. It is freeing yourself from the prison you are kept captive in by holding on to anger and fear.

Jack Kornfield says, 'We may suffer terribly from the past while those who betrayed us are on vacation. It is painful to hate. Without forgiveness we continue to perpetuate the illusion that hate can heal our pain and the pain of others. In forgiveness we let go and find relief in our heart... letting go is not the same as aversion, struggling to get rid of something. We cannot genuinely let go of what we resist. What we resist and fear secretly follows us even as we push it away. To let go of fear and trauma, we need to acknowledge just how it is. We need to feel it fully and accept that it is so. It is as it is. Letting go begins with letting be.'

Forgiveness and judgement

Forgiveness and judgement in many ways are interlinked: in order to forgive, you have to hold back on judgement, both of yourself and others. The problem is that from an early age we learn to judge ourselves and others because of how we have been inculcated to uphold certain norms. That is the way we are socialised into society; that is the way we start to learn the story about ourselves and others. But what if sometimes the story your parents, your peers or your teachers have told you is not the right one? What if you are not really 'lazy', 'bad', 'bossy' or 'stupid'? So often we have been saddled with labels from a young age that we buy into those beliefs about ourselves and about what is acceptable in order to be part of the society we live in. These flawed beliefs can create all sorts of problems, which in the extreme can lead to depression or self-destruction in the form of addiction or crime. Furthermore, accepting the labels you've been given creates the mindset that it is you who is bad, rather than your behaviour. Understanding this distinction is the first stage of learning self-compassion.

Many years ago, Barbara, my yoga teacher, introduced me to the ideas of Don Miguel Ruiz, which I found interesting but didn't relate to at that point. Ruiz is a spiritual healer who uses ancient Toltec wisdom[1] to guide people to free themselves from their self-limiting beliefs. His book *The Four Agreements* is a not a self-help manual as such, but rather a guide to understanding how we can live our lives with greater authenticity. In it, he says that agreeing to the cultural norms of society very often leads

---

1. The Toltecs were an ancient, central-American culture. Toltec wisdom is a term coined by Don Miguel Ruiz to describe indigenous Mexican beliefs, such as the need to break free from limiting world views to live a fulfilling, authentic life.

us to judge both others and ourselves by certain standards. His 'Four Agreements' – being impeccable with your word, not taking anything personally, not making assumptions and always trying to do your best – are features not only of the wisdom of many Judeo-Christian principles, but also the esoteric wisdom of other traditions. He maintains that forgiveness is the only way to heal, and furthermore it is the key to being truly free. In discussing forgiving ourselves and others, he writes: 'We can choose to forgive because we feel compassion for ourselves. We can let go of resentment and declare "That's enough! I will no longer be the big Judge that goes against myself. I will no longer beat myself up and abuse myself. I will no longer be the victim…" You know you have forgiven someone when you see them and you no longer have an emotional reaction. When someone can touch what used to be a wound and it no longer hurts you, then you know you have truly forgiven.'

Non-judgemental justice

But the question is: how can there be justice without judgement? The whole legal system in the Western world depends on fair justice for the perpetrators of crimes and their victims. Our prisons are overflowing with those who have been found guilty of committing crimes. This is retributive justice based on crime and punishment. But there is another way and that is through non-judgemental justice. This is what Gary Zukav describes as 'the freedom of seeing what you see and experiencing what you experience without responding negatively.' Forgiving demands courage and integrity, but forgiving also does not forget, for it recognises the suffering of the past and says never again will I allow these things to happen.

I have read several incredible stories of families of murder victims who have shown compassion towards the perpetrators of the crimes. It is an act of healing for them that creates a positive outcome not a negative one. They are forgiving but not forgetting. They are not holding on to the hate that so often binds people to their past, that holds them in the perpetual agony of thinking about what could have been. They are letting go and moving forward in their lives by trying to build something positive out of tragedy. They come to understand that in most cases it is not the person that is evil, it is the act they committed. They are separating the person from their behaviour, focusing on what they have done, not who they are. This is the first step in learning compassion, and it is known as restorative justice, which focuses on rehabilitation of the offenders through a reconciliation with the victims and the community. That is what redemption and atonement is about, forgiveness to allow reflection and growth. But never underestimate the courage and integrity required of the victims who undertake this.

The Truth and Reconciliation Commission set up by Nelson Mandela in South Africa is an example of non-judgemental justice, which is restorative justice. This commission had the power to grant an amnesty to those who committed abuses during the apartheid era and was a crucial component of the transition to full and free democracy in the country. This form of reconciliation is a healing process which requires the truth to be shared publicly and apologies to be made, as well as the acknowledgement and commemoration of the past injustices. This is in contrast to the Nuremberg Trials where Nazi perpetrators faced retributive justice, where there were no apologies and no amnesties. Some crimes are just too difficult to forgive; but there are many Holocaust survivors who nonetheless chose to move forward with their lives without the weight of hatred and the desire for revenge. This acceptance of reality is not a form of defeat, but rather an act of defiance. Yes, you did this to me. But I will not allow what you did to define or control my life. The perpetrators were judged, found guilty and punished, but for many of the victims, even if they did not forgive their captors, they were able to let go of their past and move forward with their lives.

In Judaism, Yom Kippur, the Day of Atonement, is the holiest day of the year. Jews fast and pray, spending twenty-five hours reflecting on their past year's misdemeanours and asking for forgiveness, for the chance to start again with a clean slate. This is all made possible by the concept of *teshuvah*, which is generally translated as 'repentance', but which literally means 'return'. It encompasses the idea that by acknowledging and confessing our past transgressions with a will to change ourselves for the better, God will forgive us. It affirms the Jewish belief that our past does not determine our future and that the sin is not the whole individual. I am not the sum total of my sin and will never be eternally damned. There is always room for change and transformation. But you can only expect to be forgiven if you have asked the people you have wronged for forgiveness. Our relationship with others is a reflection of our relationship with God.

There is a very basic principle in Judaism called *don l'kaf zechut*, which means to give someone the benefit of the doubt. The underlying notion is that one should not judge another person until you have been in their position, until you understand where they are coming from. I have tried in my life neither to offend nor judge others, always trying to give people the benefit of the doubt. But there have been occasions when I misjudged a person or a situation, which meant I needed to ask forgiveness for what I had done. One example comes to mind immediately and I realise now is that it is so deeply etched into my psyche because at the time it disturbed me greatly.

It was a family celebration and a jester had been hired to entertain the crowd during an outdoor reception. He was dressed like an ordinary guest but displayed loud, unruly behaviour as if he were drunk and constantly falling down. We happen to have a few doctors in our family, and of course they rushed over to help when this happened, only to be told it was a joke. This was repeated several times during the evening and I became increasingly upset as he was unsettling the guests. I went over to the hostess to ask her to tell him to go home, that it was enough, but she was happy to let him continue. In the end I walked up to him and shouted at him that he needed to leave. Eventually he did.

This all happened a few weeks before Yom Kippur and it weighed on my mind, because at the end of the day it was (a) not my place to intervene, and (b) I had shamed him in public by shouting at him. I then did something I had never done before to someone who in reality I didn't know at all: I found his phone number and called to ask him to forgive me for what I had done. How could I ask God for forgiveness if I had this weighing on my conscience? The jester was quite taken aback when I called and said of course he didn't mind, it was all part of his job. But the relief I felt was palpable. By forgiving me I felt that he had released me from the trap my mind was in, the guilt I felt, the self-recrimination.

But there have been other occasions when I was the one who needed to forgive. My family and I were completely overwhelmed by just how many people, some of whom we were not close to, shared with us their grief when Johnny passed away. However, there were others who perhaps we did think would be supportive, perhaps not at the time but afterwards, who did not step up to the plate. Maybe I was being judgemental, but it in some ways it hurt. I realised that I could not be judge and jury on why they failed to reach out to me, and decided that they must have had their reasons, and I had to let go of the grudge I was holding against them. Some people are just not good at expressing grief and others may have had bigger issues of their own; whatever it was, if I held on to that grudge it would be me who was the loser. I valued and still value their friendship and I felt in my heart that I needed to forgive them for not being the good friends I thought they were. In truth, I am not sure they even realised how I felt because I never told them. But forgiving them allowed me to feel better. By letting go of my grudge, I had given myself a gift.

I remember Johnny would sometimes come back from *shul* on Shabbat and say to me: 'You know so-and-so didn't greet me like he usually does,' and he would get upset about it. I would tell him that maybe something is going on in this person's life right now that we don't know about, something that is troubling him and causing him to be distracted. As the saying goes, you never know what goes on behind closed doors. I do try to give people the benefit of the doubt and not to judge them, but this is not always easy to do, especially if I feel deeply aggrieved by them. My mother was a role model in teaching me how to give people the benefit of the doubt. It's not that she ever spelled out to us in black and white that it is wrong to judge others. Rather, through her actions – she never gossiped about others or judged them – she taught by example.

Self-forgiveness

Perhaps the deepest and most important type of forgiveness is learning to forgive yourself. Lives can be upended far more by judgement than they can by disease. And self-judgement can be the most detrimental of all. When you judge others and indeed yourself, you are holding them and yourself up to some kind of impossible standard. You are seeking approval in some form to fit in with the norms of society and become admired. If you are on the receiving end of constant judgement by your family, your peers and work colleagues, it begins to gnaw away at your soul. Whatever you do will never be good enough, because you feel that not only should you do things differently, but you should be someone different. It begins in childhood and can carry on throughout your life if you accept those self-limiting beliefs that others impose on you. This anguish can lead to so many disorders – both physical and mental. So be wary of self-judgement.

Yet sometimes self-judgement can lead to self-improvement. You may admire a person of standing in the community who is a virtuous character, and therefore by trying to emulate them you are seeking to refine your own character. But this can become a slippery slope when, down the road you realise you cannot attain the same high standards, it can turn into self-condemnation.

Very often, you subconsciously hide away a part of yourself in order not to be judged. By constantly seeking the approval of others, such as posting your 'wonderful' life on social media, you are expending a large amount of energy on editing yourself to fit an image that you feel others will love. As a result, you neglect your true self in an effort to conform to others' perceptions of you. By forgiving yourself, you reclaim who you are and recognise that no one is perfect. We're all human.

During the Corona pandemic, this duality of human nature has come to the fore. Fear of catching the disease. Courage of medical professionals. Generosity of our neighbours. Selfishness of panic buyers. Vulnerability of older and ill members of society. Strength of character of so many volunteers in the community. We have learnt to value the best of humanity and I hope we have tried to forgive those who did not get it right. We need to accept that we are capable of both good and bad, and we must not hide away those parts of ourselves that we feel will not meet with universal approval.

Healing comes when you acknowledge what you have hidden away, when you accept yourself as you are and show self-compassion. But being compassionate to yourself does not mean you need to feel sorry for yourself, going into victim mode. In order to change and heal, you need to practise self-approval and self-acceptance. Self-approval begins when you accept yourself as you are in this present moment, show compassion to yourself and stop being so critical, with the understanding that you are a work in progress.

When you let go of who you think you are supposed to be, you can begin to reach your authentic self. This is not always easy for it means being both vulnerable and courageous. It means acknowledging that you are imperfect, yet allowing for self-compassion so that you can continue to face life with the strength of knowing that how are at this moment in time is exactly enough. Allowing yourself to accept the gift of forgiveness opens you up, removing any judgemental feelings you have. This will enable you to let go and move forward, heal wounds that may have festered and set you free to welcome joy and gratitude back into your life.

Stepping
Stones

Lessons I have learnt about the gift of forgiveness and the release of letting go

- Forgiveness is a prerequisite for any type of healing to take place.
- Letting go of a grudge is not the same as giving in. It is a freeing you from the prison you are kept in by holding on to your past.
- In order to forgive sometimes you have to hold back on judgement.
- Non-judgemental justice requires courage and integrity.
- Self-forgiveness releases you from unnecessary guilt and allows you to accept yourself as being enough as you are in the present moment.

Pathway Nine
The Healing Power of Food

'When diet is wrong medicine is of no use.
When diet is correct medicine is of no need.'

— AYURVEDIC PROVERB

DIARY ENTRY: *August 2018, Netanya*

What a find – a local vegan chef who cooks with fresh organic ingredients grown on a farm nearby. Gil has come to my rescue as I was wondering how I would manage spending four weeks out here with my family, who don't all really follow my organic, mainly vegan, lifestyle. But they have supported my dietary choices and lifestyle changes since cancer overtook my life, as they know that because of these additions to my life, I feel more confident about my health. However, that doesn't mean I would ask them to cook for me. I don't quite have the strength yet for doing all the necessary sourcing of ingredients and cooking all the food, so finding Gil has been such a help. He came to us, bringing all the right ingredients, and set to work in the kitchen cooking lots of wonderful fresh, nutritious organic meals that will keep me going during my stay. I'm in heaven!

You are what you eat

The food and diet revolution that has galvanised the ordinary person to take control of what and how they eat is now very much a part of our everyday lives. Yet it is difficult to know which diet to follow because there are so many differences of opinions about the efficacy of certain diets in treating specific ailments.

Much of the advice I followed about optimum diets and life-styles did not come from my medical teams but from other sources. However, it can be overwhelming trying to find information on what is best. How do you decide what advice to follow? Of course, recommendations are always important, and people who had walked this path before me or who knew others that had were usually the best source. Sophie Sabbage's *The Cancer Whisperer* has several recommendations with regard to diet, exercise and many other lifestyle recommendations. One of the other key books that has been a wonderful source of information about diet, as well as other cancer-related issues, is Dr David Servan-Schreiber's *Anti Cancer: A New Way of Life*, a book I referred to earlier. The hardback edition has a wonderful colour supplement in the middle, with graphics illustrating the best foods to prevent, and help heal the body from, cancer (the paperback edition has a shortened version). A medical doctor who twice dealt with brain cancer and investigated so much of the science behind its causes and possible cures, Dr Servan-Schreiber states that cancer cells lie within every single one of us, yet not everyone will develop cancer.

He says: 'All research on cancer concurs: genetic factors contribute to at most 15% of mortalities from cancer. In short there is no genetic fatality. We can all learn to protect ourselves.' From the outset he writes that 'without the best of conventional Western medicine including surgery, chemotherapy, radiotherapy and immunotherapy and [the new field of] molecular genetics... it is almost impossible to actually cure cancer.' It may be impossible to cure cancer without conventional medicine, but – and this is the big caveat – if 85% of cancers are not genetic then they must be environmental, from both outside and inside of our bodies. And in that case we can all try to prevent cancer from developing.

Diet and lifestyle are key issues when it comes to how and why cancer and so many other illnesses develop. The immune systems that help our bodies prevent and overcome disease depend on the immune cells operating at their optimum. As Dr Servan-Schreiber writes: '[immune cells] ... are at their best when our diets are healthy, our environment is "clean" and our physical activity involves the entire body.' However, many medical professionals, unless they specifically work in the field of nutrition, have had little training in the effect of food on the body. I conducted a straw poll of a dozen doctors among my family and friends to see just how much training in nutrition any of them had had during their student years. Not surprisingly, those aged over fifty had very little. However, those under forty had spent maybe a few weeks covering the topic. Still, a few weeks to cover what is probably one of the most important factors, apart from stress, affecting the majority of chronic conditions is very little.

I shouldn't have been surprised though, because so much of what I had read and experienced up to that point underlined the fact that the medical world of doctors, hospitals and research is focused on illness as opposed to wellness. Billions are spent on finding cures, and only a fraction of that is spent on prevention; it just doesn't add up or make sense. Big Pharma, i.e. all the pharmaceutical companies, pour millions into research on new drugs in order to make millions selling their products. Yes, many of these drugs are truly lifesaving, and I would not be here without some of them, but many of them do not have a huge impact on prolonging life, and only make patients addicted to them and have serious side effects; just think of what is going on with the opiate crisis. As one doctor famously coined, 'we have a pill for every ill.' You can't patent broccoli, green tea or turmeric, or any other type of food or nutritional supplement; if there's no money in it, there is little or no research done. Nourishing the body with the right type of food and nutrition comes not only under prevention, but in many cases it can even provide a cure to chronic conditions.

If you go to some of the cancer information websites today, they will all recommend a balanced diet, which is all well and good, but very few of them tell you to avoid processed foods, which can contain dangerous carcinogenic additives and toxins, or those with added sugar. Numerous scientific studies show that cancer cells thrive on sugar. The whole scanning procedure in PET/CT scans to detect cancer depends on the presence of sugar uptake by cancer cells. Yet you will not find the advice to steer clear of sugar in most hospital diet guidelines for cancer patients. Due to the intense chemotherapy before my stem cell transplant, and my inability to eat properly afterwards, I lost over twenty kilos. I was constantly encouraged to eat foods high in sugar and carbohydrates to help me regain my weight and give me strength to recover. How ironic, when sugar is the very thing that should be an anathema to any patient trying not only to recover from cancer, but to prevent it recurring. Giving up sugar in my diet was one of the first things I did, and although it took me a while to adjust to drinking my green tea without sugar or sweetener in it (I decided to go cold turkey), it has been worth it. Keeping away from cakes, biscuits and chocolate has not been easy because I love all of them and have always had a bit of a sweet tooth, but once you stop adding sugar to your drinks you begin to lose that sweet tooth and it becomes easier to avoid.

Cancer rates since World War II have increased significantly and this correlates with three major factors that have disrupted our environment since then: the increase in the consumption of refined sugar, the changes in farming methods and the exposure to new chemical products. All of these issues affect our food production; what and how we eat. Back in 1997, Dr Andrew Weil, whose book *Spontaneous Healing* I referred to earlier, published his book *8 Weeks to Optimum Health*. In it he addresses so many of the diet and lifestyle issues that need to be overcome in order to help the body heal. In many ways, the book was years ahead of its time in the field of integrative medicine. Today it reads like a contemporary lifestyle book.

The other piece of general advice which is recognised by most experts dealing with nutrition and disease is to avoid foods that cause inflammation in the body. This is a huge area and I am not going to go into all the details, since it is covered in the books I recommend in the bibliography, but again it is worth noting that not much mention is made of this in any hospital literature.

My dietary background

I had always tried to keep to a balanced diet not just for myself but also for my children and Johnny, who had always been a meat and two-veg man. Although he didn't have a sweet tooth for cakes and biscuits, he had a great penchant for savoury snacks, loving anything fried, especially chips. For most people, and very much so for my husband, food is not just something with which to nourish your body, it represents the nurturing comfort of home.

I grew up in a home where my parents' Eastern European background was reflected in the dishes my mother cooked. My mother was an excellent cook, and always made us fresh meals from scratch each evening after she returned from work, although an occasional treat for her was a takeaway from Bloom's, the only kosher local restaurant at the time. She didn't believe in freezers and I have memories of her busy cooking in the kitchen at two o'clock in the morning on the day before many Jewish festivals.

In the 1960s and '70s, the relationship between diet and health was not examined in the same way it is today. As I mentioned earlier, doctors at that time were not taught much about what constitutes a healthy diet, or the relationship between food and disease. Some traditional Jewish dishes such as chicken soup, which is known as the Jewish penicillin, and fermented sauerkraut and beetroot, are now referred to as 'superfoods' with health benefits, but many of the recipes back then were based on fried foods and animal fats, so not the healthiest in today's terms. One of my abiding memories is of my father spreading lashings of *schmaltz*, which is the collected fat from cooked chickens and geese, on his bread before eating it topped with slices of salami. Literally a heart attack on a plate, but I have to say it did taste good!

When I married, much of my cooking was based on what I had seen my mother cook and was commonplace in our social circles. One of these dishes, which sums up both the nurturing aspect of food and its cultural background, is chulent, a dish made with beans, barley, meat and root vegetables, which was one of Johnny's favourites. Actually, if you leave out the meat and animal fat, it is quite healthy. Johnny was immensely proud of my cooking, and not one Shabbat went by without him savouring the delights of my chulent, a dish kept warm overnight to avoid the prohibition of cooking on Shabbat. Such was his particularity about the dish that it could not be served as accompaniment to the main meal but had to be served as a separate course in a soup bowl. I could fill a whole book with the delights of my home cooking and the favourite dishes of each member of my family but suffice to say, food did play a significant role in our family life.

Many years ago, after reading Andrew Weil's book, I did try to move the family on to a more vegetarian-based diet, but with three growing boys and a hardworking husband, it was difficult to keep them satisfied. And like so many things that interested me and I read up on at the time, it was something I dipped in and out of, but it didn't become a total change in lifestyle. In the 1970s and '80s, vegetarianism was part of the hippy heritage; veganism and the type of healthy eating that is so commonplace now was very much considered a 'fringe' cuisine back then. I remember my sister-in-law Jamie, who is a nutritionist from Los Angeles, giving me a gift of a cookery book over thirty-five years ago called *The Enchanted Broccoli Forest*. All the recipes were vegetarian and I had never heard of half the ingredients ... tofu, soy oil, tamari sauce, millet, turmeric. Yet today, not only are these standard products available in any grocery store, but their health benefits are widely understood.

Macrobiotics

The turning point for me came around fifteen years ago when I found out about a vegetarian cookery course being run at a friend's house. I signed up for it, thinking this was what I had been waiting for: guidance on how to cook and eat more healthily. What I hadn't realised was that the woman teaching the classes was not just an ordinary vegetarian cook, but a macrobiotic chef. Macrobiotics, as I would soon learn, was not just a way of cooking food but a way of eating and living in harmony with oneself and one's environment, that has profound healing effects on a person's health. By eating whole, living, natural foods in season, we can help our bodies recover from so many of the imbalances that cause disease. The founding principle of macrobiotics, the idea that each person is responsible for their own life and health, was totally radical when it was first developed. Like other ideas and philosophies that originate from the Far East, it is also about balancing the body's energies, ideas that were pioneered there years ago, but which only became mainstream in the West towards the end of the twentieth century.

I am not going to delve into the principles and framework of the macrobiotic diet, but I think it will help to just mention some of the foods it covers. Firstly, although in season organic vegetables and fruit are at the core of many of the dishes and should make up between 40–50% of your daily intake, it is not a vegetarian diet per se, since fish is also permitted. Whole grains, dried beans, seeds, nuts and fermented foods are all constituents of the diet, which aims to balance acid and alkaline-forming foods. Other foods such as sea vegetables (different types of seaweed) and all forms of soya, such as miso, tempeh and tofu, are also key ingredients in macrobiotic dishes. To anyone accustomed to the standard fare of roast chicken, shepherd's pie and meatballs, this may all sound very foreign, but once you are shown how to cook the dishes and understand the system it is based on, it becomes much more attractive.

Macrobiotic cooking was another example of a lifestyle I tried to get into but didn't fully adopt. That changed when I began my cancer treatment. A friend of the family in New York recommended a book written by a woman she knew personally, who had cured her aggressive lung and bone cancer by turning herself entirely over to macrobiotics, working with a shiatsu practitioner and adopting many of the associated lifestyle choices that come with macrobiotics. Elaine Nussbaum's story of her recovery from cancer could seem like a fluke to some, just like the exceptional patients described by Bernie Siegel. Yet I recognised the connection between Elaine's story and what I had been taught in the cookery classes. I didn't fully make the change after reading Elaine Nussbaum's book, *Recovery from Cancer*, but I explored the ideas further. Then a year later, when my cancer transformed into a high-grade aggressive lymphoma and I read Sophie Sabbage's book, I knew it was time for me to get serious in my approach to healing. I understood that if I was going to adopt a macrobiotic diet and its associated lifestyle, I would need some help.

It was at this point that I was about to learn a very important lesson about finding the right people to work with, because I found someone who was most definitely not the right person. I was recommended a woman who was a macrobiotic expert and to say that she was unusual and had a totally different take on life was an understatement. She was totally committed to a macrobiotic lifestyle and felt everyone could benefit from it. However, after just a few sessions with her I realised that although I understood the benefits of living like that, it would have a huge impact not only on what I ate, but also on my social life and lifestyle. She insisted that I should eat my own food before going out to any restaurant or friend's house, for it would be unlikely they would cook the macrobiotic food I needed to eat. As you can imagine, this was not a desirable option. She also worked on my body with shiatsu massage which was very strong and usually resulted days later in a urine infection! Her methods were just too extreme for me to maintain on a long-term basis, and so our association came to an end after a few months.

However, there were good things that came from our encounters. I was working with her during one of the most intense periods of chemotherapy after my cancer transformed to high grade. At one point, I became neutropenic when my neutrophil blood levels dropped, a very dangerous situation, and had to be hospitalised. This was a week before Johnny and I had booked to fly out to Israel for our eldest grandchild Meital's *bat mitzvah*.[1] As I lay in that hospital room, my macrobiotic woman recommended a special macrobiotic food called amazake, which, when eaten with rice, creates stabilising conditions in the body. I sent Johnny out to buy the ingredients and bring the dish to the hospital for me. The flight was booked for Wednesday and each day, I would visualise my body recovering and prayed desperately that my blood counts would recover so I could get on that plane. Whether it was the amazake or mind over matter, by Tuesday my levels had improved enough for me to be discharged. I got on that plane with my hand sanitiser and face mask (years before they would become compulsory!) and danced my heart out that weekend with the joy of being with my family at one of the biggest celebrations I had shared with them since the start of my cancer journey.

Ingredients to heal

Perhaps one of the most bizarre stories that happened to me in relation to my cancer and my diet was to do with a certain gentleman called Norman. Let me give you the background. I was trying my best to stick to my macrobiotic diet but it was proving very difficult, and I found myself craving certain foods which were not permitted according to the diet. I was eating nutritious food during the day but late in the evening I would crave a packet of crisps, some chocolate or another type of snack. It may have been partly due to the chemotherapy I was going through at the time, which included steroids that are known to increase your appetite.

---

1. A Jewish girl's confirmation at the age of twelve.

It was at this point that the dietician Lara at the Chai Cancer Care came to my rescue. I had a few sessions with her, which were not just advice on what and how to eat, but more about emotional therapy and seeing food within the framework of coping with my illness. She told me that stressing over the exact type of food I was eating could cause more damage to my body than actually eating a piece of chocolate that would satisfy me.

And in some ways, this idea relates to what I wrote earlier about the emotions of fear. How many times do you hear of people who live healthy lifestyles and exercise regularly, yet still develop cancer or some other disease? Sometimes the problem is that although they are doing everything necessary to maintain a healthy lifestyle, they are also afraid and stressed about not being able to keep up their regimes and consequently becoming ill or gaining weight from that.

Understanding that stressing about the strict controls of my diet could cause more harm than breaking the rules every now and then, helped me to modify my approach to how and what I ate. I had realised that sticking very strictly to one type of diet was not going to work for me. Although I continued with a mainly macrobiotic diet I did include other types of foods, still trying to be mainly vegetarian. This approach was also supported by the advice in Sophie Sabbage's book, where she had tried different healing diets and in the end came down to one that was 80% vegetarian and 20% fish or chicken, provided it was organic.

So back to Norman. During one of our sessions, Lara told me about a man who had created a type of juice that had been helping some of her patients. I was intrigued. She told me he managed a kosher Chinese restaurant and that he was happy to help out cancer patients as he himself had been one. It seemed like an oxymoron... the manager of a Chinese restaurant, where monosodium glutamate and all types of unhealthy, fried food were on the menu, was promoting a healthy juice to help cancer patients. But I left our session with his number and after a quick call arranged to meet him at his restaurant. It turned out that Norman's father and son were both doctors and he himself had gone through two bouts of cancer and was now in complete remission. Many years earlier he had done an enormous amount of research into the efficacy of certain foods in preventing and curing cancer. After telling me his cancer story, and how he came to create his juice, he went on to demonstrate how to make it with the help of one of the waiters in the restaurant.

GREEN JUICE

INGREDIENTS (IDEALLY ORGANIC)

2 cucumbers
1 head of broccoli
1 bunch of black grapes
3 fingers of fresh turmeric

METHOD

Juice the cucumber, broccoli and turmeric (if possible, use a masticating juicer which gives the best results). Blend the grapes (you need the skin and seeds of these so don't juice them) in a nutribullet or similar blender. Mix the two together and stir well.

This should make about one litre of juice. Drink half first thing in the morning and the other half in the late afternoon. For the initial three months after diagnosis and during treatment, drink this twice a day, every day. Then after things stabilise, drink it just two days a week.

All the ingredients are natural, everyday foods which aren't expensive so there is not much cost involved other than, if you do not have them already, buying a blender and a juicer. I was in the middle of chemotherapy and it was quite a business to get started with buying all the ingredients and making the juice every day, but I wanted to try to give myself the best chance to help my body. So I set about this and started on my green juice supplements, which four years later I am still taking twice a week. Subsequent to my meeting with him, I found out about some other cancer patients who had been following his advice and who were doing very well. He told me he now spends much of his time on the phone to clients from all around the world, who by word-of-mouth from surviving cancer patients found out about his juice. He does not charge a penny for his time and advice and says he just wants to help people. So far, supplementing my diet with the juice seems to be helping me but I feel it's just part of what I call my Tesco motto approach to dealing with all types of treatments, supplements and advice – 'every little helps.'

There is so much advice out there about the types of foods and supplements that can help you through your cancer journey and indeed any other diseases you may be suffering from. I have used a naturopath who was recommended to me and at times have taken different concoctions of herbs to drink and make up various teas. I started along the vitamin route, and one thing that the medical world does advise is to take a Vitamin D3 supplement, which I do every day. A friend of mine who had been undergoing cancer treatment suggested the Golden Milk recipe below to drink every day. I started drinking this after reading about the benefits of turmeric, not just for curing cancer but for a whole variety of ailments. Once you get the hang of making it, the whole thing only takes ten minutes to prepare.

GOLDEN MILK

INGREDIENTS (IDEALLY ORGANIC)

1½ cups filtered or spring water
½ cup turmeric powder
½ cup filtered or spring water
½ teaspoon ground black pepper
½ teaspoon ground cinnamon
1 teaspoon ginger powder
¼ teaspoon salt
½ cup raw organic coconut oil

METHOD

Place 1½ cups of water in a pan with ½ cup turmeric powder. Bring to a slow simmer, stirring continuously. When it begins to thicken add the other ½ cup of water with the rest of the spices. Bring back to a slow simmer and stir for 5–6 minutes or until it thickens to a paste. Take off the heat and stir in the coconut oil and keep stirring until it is completely melted. Pour into a jar and leave to cool completely. Give one last stir to make sure the coconut oil is properly incorporated and put in the fridge. It should last 2–3 weeks.

TO MAKE THE GOLDEN MILK

Heat a cup of milk of your choice (almond is my favourite), pour 1 teaspoon of the paste over the hot milk. If you want to sweeten it, add a bit of honey.

In a way, what I had been doing over the years, blending Western and Eastern medical traditions, I was now doing with my cuisine. And this reflects so much of what I now espouse as the best advice for people going through cancer or any other illness. You have to find what works for you, research the different suggestions and combine different methods to create a framework in which you can both live comfortably and feel that you are helping your body to heal.

Today's food is suffused with different cultures, from Japanese sushi bars to Chinese and Indian restaurants, Italian pizza stores and the like. Yet although there are many foods from all of these traditions that are tasty and readily available, not all of them are healing foods. Much also depends on the preparation methods, and sources of where and how the food is grown. Many of the dishes are prepared in a fast-food environment and while they are definitely fast foods, they are not healing foods. The saying: 'Let food be your medicine or medicine will become your food,' is an idea that has been taken very seriously in the East for many hundreds of years. There have been numerous studies about the different cancer rates among Mediterranean countries, the Far East and the West. So many of them have shown that the diets of certain countries are often the key to understanding why some cancers are less prolific in different cultures.

To be honest, I have no idea which key ingredients work better for me than others when it comes to the food I eat and the supplements I use. I know that I have made sure and investigated that what I eat is not harmful and that according to knowledgeable opinions, all the different foods I eat and products I use can help. I cannot categorically prove the efficacy of any of them other than what I have read about in terms of the success of using certain products. What I do know is that I feel better and so far, thank God, my cancer has stabilised. Yes, I have had serious medical interventions without which I don't think I would still be alive. But there is being alive and surviving and there is being alive and healthily thriving, and I hope I am 'healthier' now because I've been nourish myself with healthy food as part of my healing journey.

Stepping Stones

Lessons I have learnt about the healing power of food

- There is a proven relationship between diet and disease.
- The type of food we eat and the way it has been grown and processed can influence the functioning of our immune system.
- While it is difficult to scientifically prove the health benefits of certain foods due to lack of research, this should not discourage you from trying out different diets and foods.
- Be patient and creative about exploring different diets and finding what will work for you without inducing stress.
- Much of the evidence comes from Eastern medicine which has known the benefits of certain foods for hundreds of years.

Pathway Ten

Faith is Not Just for
the Religious

'Faith is the force of life. If man lives then he must believe in something.'
— LEO TOLSTOY

DIARY ENTRY: *August 2016*

Almost there. I am almost done with my last chemotherapy treatment which we hope will finally bring me the remission I need. And it's my sixtieth birthday in two days' time. I often ask God if He could grant me just enough years for Johnny and me to see our grandchildren grow up and meet all our yet unborn ones. Over the past four years, as my cancer kept returning, I thought that my faith would be strong enough to keep me going. In many ways it has, but there have been moments when I have had my doubts. I think of my father who lived through the hell of the Holocaust yet went faithfully every week to shul praying to a God who was absent from his life when he came face-to-face with the angel of death in the camps. If he could still talk to God, how can I give up? I have been so blessed in my life but feel that maybe my good fortune is running out. Yet I won't stop asking God for a reprieve, for hopefully He is listening and His answer will be a positive one.

There is an expression in Hebrew 'acharon acharon chaviv', which loosely translates to mean that the very last one is the most beloved, or as one might express colloquially in English, last but not least. And so it is with my healing pathways. I could have filled this whole book with references to Jewish sources both biblical and philosophical, and I have discussed these in a few places. But this is not a religious thesis or a book about religion and philosophy, and I am certainly not an expert in either. However, just as when I wrote about love I used the idea of being guided by it, so too in many ways the guiding light in my life has been my Jewish faith.

Courage to live with uncertainty

One does not need to be religious to have faith. You do not have to be a practising Christian, Muslim, Hindu, Jew or Buddhist to have faith, for although it can mean adhering to a certain set of rules or holding a given set of beliefs, to me having faith is just as much to do with connecting to something outside of yourself, as it is about following a specific codification of how to live your life. By connecting to a spiritual framework of some kind, one recognises that life is more than just the physical world we live in; life itself is the connectedness of all living things and faith is what lifts humanity to a place where this is acknowledged.

Rabbi Sacks gave perhaps the most succinct and significant description of what having faith means. He says it is the courage to live with uncertainty knowing that the future is unpredictable. It is 'not the absence of doubt, but the ability to recognise doubt and still take the risk of commitment.' These words, particularly the courage one needs to live with the unpredictability of life, have deeply resonated with me throughout all the challenges that I have had to face in recent years. Courage is often something that you don't know you possess until you are faced with a situation that calls for it. It takes courage to admit you're vulnerable and not everyone wants to or has the ability to do so. Having faith helps you move forward with courage because you feel you are not alone, and

I don't mean that in a physical sense, but more in a metaphysical and spiritual sense.

Whether your belief is in one God, in some form of universal being or an energy source to which we are all connected, that sense of connectivity to something outside of ourselves that cannot be seen or very often understood, but is sensed deep within, gives one an inner strength and resolve. And it is this strength that is needed to help us heal, through the resilience we build for ourselves. But there is more to having faith than just having courage and connection. It is also the ability to hold hope in your heart. Hope is the greatest gift that any form of faith can bestow. And it is the hope of recovery and the hope of better times to come that have been perhaps the most important stepping stones on my healing journey.

Faith, as practised through my religion and through my spiritual connection to all that is, has kept me going through some of my darkest times and has brought light into that darkness by allowing me to reconnect to so many things that make life worth living. I have lived all my life as a practising orthodox Jew, yet my faith in God and my conversations with Him are not just within the framework of daily prayers and religious rituals. At times when I feel a depth of inner gratitude I look upwards and whisper a silent thank you to the heavens above. Likewise, when I feel angry, I sometimes direct that rage to God, and yes I have had many of those conversations too.

The Hebrew word for faith is *emunah* and this has a double connotation for me. My faith, my Judaism, has been the bedrock of how I have lived my life. Emunah is also the name of the social welfare organisation that I have been involved in over the last thirty-five years, both in the UK and in Israel, and that has brought deep meaning to my life. My faith has not only given me a framework for my relationship with God, but it is the basis of the relationships I have with others. By helping those less fortunate than my family, I found an added purpose in my life and a commitment to something bigger than myself. As David Brooks writes in *The Second Mountain*, commitments not only give us our identity, they give us a sense of purpose and build our character. The Emunah organisation was established to provide a safe haven for Holocaust refugees more than eighty years ago. Having met so many of the children and families that it has helped, I know just what a difference it has made to their lives, and still does today, helping so many at-risk and disadvantaged children. This is what faith does; it gives you a perspective outside of yourself, it creates a framework for the ethics of responsibility. In the words of Rabbi Sacks, 'Faith is a form of listening... for the responsible life is one that responds.'

I read a beautiful explanation about the root of the Hebrew word for faith, *emunah*. Eti Shani, a Hebrew language teacher, explains that although faith is often connected to religion, the root of the word is actually *em*, which means 'mother', a person who is an influence in our lives, subconsciously guiding and nurturing us. The explanation below is from Eti Shani's website, hebrew.learnoutlive. com, and it sums up so wonderfully the essence of faith.

> The Hebrew word for faith is Emunah (אמונה). We usually think of faith as something which is connected to (organized) religion and may have many preconceived notions about it, but when we look at the root it might turn out to be something far more primal to our existence.
>
> The word Emunah is based on the word Em (אם) which means mother. Like a mother who is feeding, teaching and loving her child, Emunah is an almost subconscious influence in our life that nurtures us and gently guides us in our journey through this world.
>
> Most of us turn towards this sense of faith only during hard moments, hanging our hopes on a higher power that will help us overcome a certain difficulty or crisis and then we immediately tend to forget it when everything is fine again.
>
> Whether we are aware of it or not is irrelevant, however, since this sense of faith is always already there, like a fetus

inside the womb is also not aware of the mother's existence, and yet she constantly provides for all its needs. The Hebrew word for womb is rechem (רחם) which shares the same letters with the word mercy (רחמים – rachamim), meaning that like a fetus grows in a mother's womb, we grow here in this world in a surrounding influence of mercy. In other words, there's a hidden aspect of life which always supports and nurtures us, giving us exactly what we need at the right moment and in the right portion. Although we may not always be in agreement with the general conditions of any given moment in time, the sense of faith is what aligns us with the intent of goodness behind these conditions.

It's like when sometimes in life we desperately want something specific to happen which refuses to occur and only many years later we are grateful that things didn't go our way, because we realize it wasn't what we needed. This realization is an aspect of mercy.

Instead of going through constant cycles of desperation, frustration and waiting for the realization many years later, faith is a way to experience this completeness in each and every moment. Students of Hebrew will know that the word for 'complete' (שלם – shalem) shares the same root with the word for 'peace' (שלום – shalom), i.e. inner peace is a sense of completeness.

After all, as the old sages say, if already a human mother here in this world cares for a child and wants only the best for it, how much vaster is this caring and compassion in a spiritual sense?...[these ideas show us]...that our life is not something to be managed, to be 'good at,' or to 'be figured out,' but a journey towards gently coming into contact with this origin of love, hope and completeness.

Faith in my upbringing

I have been firmly on this journey of faith and love since my cancer diagnosis and the death of my husband. But that is not to say that faith was not part of my life growing up. Faith for me came first and foremost in a practical way as our family always kept the Jewish laws and followed the belief system that it entailed. Most children in their early years believe what they are told by their parents to be true and if their lifestyles reflect those beliefs, they will usually grow up accepting them without too much questioning, until an age when they are capable to think things through for themselves. Being raised in a religious home as I was, in my early years it was taken as a given. It was something I imbibed along with chicken soup. Observing Shabbat, the Jewish festivals and the kosher dietary laws were part of the fabric of my life. And the rituals that were so much a part of that life were by and large celebrated with love and joy, not compulsion or enforcement. The rituals gave a focus to our gatherings with family and friends, which were often noisy, joyous affairs.

Questioning one's upbringing and rebelling against the social norms one lives within usually comes in the teenage years or later, when one is trying find one's place in the world and making sense of everything. My parents were fortunate in that I never really rebelled; I never felt the need to. I had a strong network of family and friends, all of us living the religious life, and after spending my gap year in Israel my attachment to my Judaism only grew stronger. Up until that time my understanding of faith was always within the context of religion. I didn't fully appreciate that the practices I kept and the rituals I participated in had expanded my world. I had wonderful experiences in the religious youth clubs I attended, both the local Sinai youth club and Bnei Akiva, a large international youth organisation. Their weekly meetings, ongoing activities in the community and the summer camps they ran were an integral part of my childhood and teenage years. Indeed, as I mentioned previously, my gap year was on the Bnei Akiva Hachshara scheme.

Participating in collective rituals makes you as an individual part of something bigger than yourself, and it enriches you in so many ways that you often don't fully understand or appreciate at the time. Looking back, I realise that much of my social and organisational skills were developed while participating in those youth clubs, learning both a sense of what it means to be part of a group, and later as a leader of that group, understanding the obligations and importance of what that entails. Social responsibility, comprehending the virtues and values within society, creates a framework in which faith thrives by the commitment you give to others. If you absorb these experiences from a young age, they stay with you for life.

My love affair with Israel

But it was in Israel that the groundwork for my future life was mapped out, both in a religious and a spiritual sense. As the daughter of a Holocaust survivor, I knew that Israel was the only place where Jewish people could truly feel safe and at home both physically and spiritually. Working on a kibbutz, touring the country to spending time studying Jewish texts, all stirred within me a deep-seated love of the land, the people and the religion that were part of my heritage. There were times during my year there when I felt closer to God than at any other time previously, as it gave me a physical bond to my religion which deepened my faith and spiritual connection. The honest truth is that my love affair with Israel was born during that year and it has continued ever since.

Johnny always used to say that his *neshamah*, his soul, felt at home whenever he was in Israel; he felt his whole being was at peace in a way that he couldn't quite explain, but knew was different to how he felt in London or anywhere else in the world. He had also spent a year on a kibbutz after finishing high school and had spent countless hours working in the fields, which connected him intimately with the land. Today it is the country where three of my children and all my grandchildren now live and the place where, eventually, I hope to live out my retirement years.

In a way it is hardly surprising that my year in Israel influenced me so deeply in a spiritual sense. My experience of God until then had largely centred around attending synagogue services, which during the 1960s were not inspiring for young children. In addition, having attended a non-Jewish secondary school, my teenage Jewish education was limited to the inadequate *cheder* – afterschool Jewish education – system that existed in synagogues in the 1960s and '70s. This is so unlike the incredible Jewish education system that now exists, not only in Jewish primary and secondary schools in the UK, but in the plethora of informal education opportunities in virtually every synagogue and community centre.

Even when I was in a Jewish primary school, we were taught to translate *chumash*, the text of the Torah, by rote. Although we learnt the Hebrew alphabet and could read Hebrew, we left school unable to speak the living language. So yes, hardly an inspiring induction to the unbelievably rich sources of the Jewish faith. That induction came while I was in Israel, when studying Jewish sources resonated with me in a deeper way. And so began my thirst to learn so much more about the religion I lived and practised every day. It would eventually lead me to embark on a master's degree in Jewish Studies, which not only enriched my knowledge of the incredible canon of Jewish religious texts, but also gave me a deeper understanding of my faith.

There are numerous stories in the Torah that illustrate the power of faith, but as I wrote earlier, I am not going to delve into this subject other than to say that many of them, such as the story of Ruth the Moabite, illustrate the power of kindness to redeem tragedy and bring joy. The very word 'ruthless,' which is an antonym to kindness, demonstrates the power of this story. Ruth went on to become the grandmother of the greatest king of Israel, David.

In the past eight years, since my cancer diagnosis and the death of Johnny, I have not only thought more deeply about what having faith means to me, but also about the wider implications of spiritual connections that have opened my awareness to so many things. It is this heightened awareness that has helped my healing, guiding me to a more profound understanding of the meaning and purpose in my life, giving me a direction and helping me to find peace. When things were really difficult, it was my faith that kept me going.

But having faith does not mean that you sit back and pray that all will turn out OK, leaving God or the universal energies to come together to work it all out for you. On the contrary. There is an extremely important concept in Judaism called *hishtadlut*, which literally translates as 'effort' or 'endeavour', but its true meaning is encapsulated in the idiom 'God helps those who help themselves.' My mother, who was an incredibly religious person and, as I wrote earlier, not in the sense that she sat praying all day long, but in her deep faith in God, was an enormous believer in this. She taught all of us, and all our children and grandchildren, the importance of putting in the effort to succeed, and then God will help you. Healing from any trauma or challenge requires such a mindset. You cannot truly heal by being passive. You have to be active and take charge of the process; you have put in the effort to find out what works for you and then carry it out to the best of your ability.

But this was not easy for my children, especially having to deal with the double blow of my illness and then the death of their father. Unlike my parents, and many of their generation who survived the horrors of the war and who tried to protect their children from any distress, Johnny and I had been totally open with our children every step of the way through my illness. They understood the implications of each treatment and my chances of survival. With three of them and their families living in Israel, they had the added burden of constantly flying back and forth for visits. There was even a time after my stem cell transplant when they were all suddenly summoned to London, to say their goodbyes to me, as I was in intensive care and the doctors didn't think I would make it. How they kept their faith through it all I don't know, but what I do know is they didn't share their fears or doubts with me. They were the ones giving me hope, giving me the courage and faith to keep fighting for my life. They were the ones who gave and still give meaning and purpose to my life.

However, after Johnny died, everything shifted and I had to be the one giving my strength out to them, holding us all up as we crumpled under the weight of our shock and grief. It was then that my faith and spiritual focus came to the fore, guiding me, empowering me to pull them and myself through it all. It wasn't easy and to this day I feel that perhaps none of us have fully processed the grief of Johnny's passing. But we are able to experience joyous moments again as a family, to reminisce about Johnny with love and laughter, to share with family and friends the good times and the difficult times in the knowledge that Johnny will forever be a part of our lives.

I know what my faith has given me, but perhaps it was my struggles that brought me to where I am now. Had I not gone through them, I don't think I would have lost my faith, but perhaps I would still be practising it and understanding it in a more mundane way. For there were times along my journey when the pathways looked like they were coming to a dead end and that there was a strong probability that things could all go horribly wrong. But this was when my faith came to the fore. As Rabbi Sacks says: 'Faith is the defeat of probability by the power of possibility; if you have faith nothing is impossible.' Without my faith perhaps I would not have had the gift of true life satisfaction that comes with knowing yourself and understanding how a spiritual life can bring you happiness in so many different ways and help you to heal.

Stepping

Lessons I have learnt about the power of faith

- Having faith acknowledges the connection to something outside of yourself and does not necessarily mean holding a given set of beliefs or upholding given rules.
- More than connection, faith generates hope.
- If participation in the rituals of faith are practised with love and not coercion, they can foster a sense of community and responsibility.

- Faith thrives in the commitment you give to others.
- Studying the basis and context of your faith can help foster a deeper understanding and meaning of its place in your life.
- Faith is about holding on to the possibilities in life.

Afterword
It's Your Choice

'Life can only be understood backwards but must be lived forwards.'
— SØREN KIERKEGAARD

Life is a journey and we all know its final destination. What we do not know is how we will reach that destination. Sometimes on a journey you have to stop and look back to appreciate just how far you have progressed along the way, and sometimes you need to look back in order to recalibrate and change direction. Discovering new pathways may help you to continue your journey in an improved physical, mental and emotional state, where you are at peace.

Yet the question remains for me – have I fully healed? I am still not sure. I think about Johnny every day, but I am learning to live and go forward without him by my side. My latest scan showed that for the time being my cancer seems to be in remission. My journey towards full health is still ongoing and I am working on my healing every day. And healing is a lifetime's work, for you can come through any challenge alive but not be fully living. The decision to live fully means you have to take an active role in your life by being fully present and having the courage to show up no matter how hard it is.

I sometimes ask myself: If I could take my body back to where it was before I had cancer, would I? Of course I would. No question.

But would I want to return to my mental, emotional and spiritual state before I was diagnosed? That is a good question. I wouldn't wish on anyone the challenges that I have had to face in recent years. But they have forced me to change in ways that I could have never foreseen. They have taken me along pathways that maybe I would not have explored if my life had just muddled along in the same familiar patterns.

Living with a life-threatening disease, followed by a sudden bereavement, as I wrote in the introduction, acted as a wakeup call to examine how I was living my life. Sometimes we live our lives as if we are sleepwalking our way through it; as if we are treading a path that is prescribed and although it can be a happy and enjoyable journey, we are not fully alive, not fully our authentic selves.

It is hard to be self-aware and dig deep into one's psyche when you are busy raising a family, struggling with work, along with a hundred other commitments that fill your life. Perhaps it's about timing too. When you reach your fifties and sixties hopefully you reach a place where, if you have children, they are settled, if not with their own families then at least they are able to look after themselves. It is an age where hopefully you have had some job satisfaction in your life and if you are lucky enough to be in good health and financially stable then you have the luxury of time to think about your life in a deeper context. But there is something more to this in that as you get older you realise how short life is and how it passes you by without you sometimes stopping to think where you are going. As it is quoted in *Pirkei Avot, The Ethics of the Fathers*: 'From where have you come and where are you going to?' Sometimes we need to remind ourselves to ask this questions.

Today many people choose to go on journeys to 'find themselves' at a younger age, specifically after high school, when they travel around the world in search of enriching experiences and new meaning in their lives. Some of them find the right answers, but many do not. The problem is that so often people know they are searching for something; they go far and wide looking, but what they often don't realise is that the answers don't lie in some faraway place but rather deep within themselves. And even if they do come to that understanding, life can get in the way and things don't always turn out the way you plan them. You end up reverting to a life of conformity rather than authenticity and this can be the underlying cause of so much stress, since there is a tension between how you want to live your life and how you are currently living your life.

Often we get so caught up in life that we put our true purpose to the side. We don't always even recognise that this is the case or that there is something missing. For me, it was two very big lifeshocks – disease and bereavement – that ended the established pattern of my life and caused me to begin anew within a different framework. They initiated in me a search to find how I could best heal myself in order to move forward. It was this process that led to the book in your hands right now.

Through all the pathways we take to help us heal, we are searching for our way home. But as Jeff Foster says in his book *The Deepest Acceptance*: 'Throughout all human history … [mankind] is seeking some kind of grand unified all-encompassing theory of reality, to find wholeness in chaos, to find love in the midst of devastation, to find cosmic closure … somehow seeking equilibrium, seeking home. All things long to come to rest. Home is not a place, a thing or a person. It is rest.'

Two thousand years ago, King David encapsulated this idea in many of his beautiful psalms: 'Return my soul to restfulness.' Rabbi Joseph B. Soloveitchik, one of the most renowned modern Jewish philosophers and scholars, wrote in his book, *Kol Dodi Dofek* (*Listen – My Beloved Knocks*), about the essence of fate and destiny as part of a discussion of the Jewish people's return to their historical homeland. His ideas of fate and destiny and how one makes choices have helped me form many of my attitudes. As he elucidates in his essay, there are certain things that happen to us that are beyond our control. What you do have control over is how you react to the situation, how you choose your attitude, for that will shape your destiny out of the hand you have been dealt.

It's not your fault if you get cancer or any other disease. Likewise, accidents that cause debilitating injuries, financial distress, relationship breakdowns and the like are not always a result of your actions. The death of a loved one may have been anticipated or may happen completely unexpectedly, forever changing the course of your life. All of these events are your fate, events out of your control. What you *do* have control over is how you react to that situation. The way you act and what path you follow – this is how you create your destiny. As much as your life may be spinning out of control, there are ways to deal with your challenges, which will create a destiny that can help you to heal, change and take you along a different path. Choosing a path and new mindset is not easy. However, I believe that if we cannot learn from our suffering, if we cannot find any meaning to it, then I feel that we have lost an opportunity that life has given us to move forward with purpose, with love and newfound joy.

Victor Frankl sums these ideas up in his most famous book, *Man's Search for Meaning*:

> 'We must never forget that we may find meaning in life even when confronted with a hopeless situation, when facing a fate that cannot be changed. For what then matters is to bear witness to the uniquely human potential at its best, which is to transform a personal tragedy into a triumph, to turn one's predicament into a human achievement... In the last resort man should not ask "What is the meaning of my life?" but should realise that he himself is being questioned. Life is putting its problems to him, and it is up to him to respond to these questions by being responsible; he can only answer to life by answering for his life. Life is a task.'

What has been my task? Why did I get ill? Why did my husband die far too early? I can't give you answers. But I am sure that I have learnt more about myself and life than I would have if I hadn't endured these challenges. Maybe that has been my task, learning to heal myself and then share with others how I have transformed my suffering into something positive; how I have gained a much deeper appreciation of the gifts that living in this world can bring us.

If I could sum up my life's philosophy now, after all that I have been through, I would do it in just twelve words:

LET GO AND FORGIVE
FEEL AND SHOW GRATITUDE
LOVE AND BE LOVED

Let go of all the things and people that irk you and practise forgiveness for yourself and for others.

Feel with gratitude and appreciation all your blessings and show gratitude to those who care for you.

Love people and open your heart to allow the love of those around you to penetrate into your soul.

No one has all the answers, but I believe that creating a mindset that encompasses what I call the Four 'A's may help: **Acknowledgement, Allowance, Attitude and Acceptance.**

You need to acknowledge and accept that your life's challenges are there for a reason. You may never discover what that reason is, but you need to answer the call by taking responsibility for the choices you make; you have to try to adopt an attitude that allows you to see the blessings that are hidden inside that challenge. If you follow these things through and open yourself up, hopefully this will help you on your healing journey.

I will leave the final quote of the book to Edith Eger because its sums up my attitude: 'Healing isn't about recovery, it's about discovery. Discovering hope in hopelessness, discovering an answer where there doesn't seem to be one, discovering that it's not what happens that matters – it's what you do with it.'

Whatever you face in life, it is up to *you* to choose how you react and move forward with the fate you have been dealt. Hopefully you will be able to choose pathways that will heal you and bring you home.

Bibliography

Writing this book was not just a therapeutic exercise for me; I hope that it will be an opportunity for you to broaden your horizons as to what is available out there to help you on your journey through whatever challenges you are facing in your life. To this end, I felt it was important not just to give a list of books that I found interesting, helpful and enjoyable, but also to add comments on what they cover and how the book can be useful. If you want to gain a taste of the authors' viewpoints, many of them have videos on YouTube.

Below is the list of books, ordered alphabetically by author.

GREGG BRADEN

The Divine Matrix – (Hay House 2007)

> The author is an internationally respected pioneer in bridging science, spirituality and the real world. This book discusses the connecting force between all living things, in understandable scientific language.

Resilience from the Heart – (Hay House 2015)

> Using his years of research into ancient wisdom and the latest biological discoveries, Braden provides a strategy for building heart-based resilience to help improve people's lives.

DAVID BROOKS

The Road to Character – (Penguin 2016)

> A powerful book written by one of America's foremost social commentators about the way that the contemporary 'me'

culture has eroded our ability to create meaningful inner lives. By describing people whose sense of humility was fundamental to their success, he shows us how in order to fulfil yourself, you must learn how to forget yourself.

The Second Mountain – (Random House 2019)

Discussing the premise that individualism has torn apart the social fabric of our communities, this book explores the path to repair by four commitments that can define a life of meaning and purpose. Our personal fulfilment depends on how well we choose and execute these.

Simon G. Brown and Dragana G. Brown

Modern Day Macrobiotics – (Carroll & Brown 2005)

A useful short book to help you understand the principles behind macrobiotics with plenty of tasty recipes.

Daniel M Davis

The Beautiful Cure: Harnessing Your Body's Natural Defences – (Vintage 2018)

Written by a leading immunologist, this book reads like a mystery novel in telling the story of the discoveries that helped our understanding of how our immune system works. It is fascinating reading which at times gets a bit technical, but it is worth ploughing through for gaining a better knowledge of the most recent new treatments for cancer, and other diseases.

Joe Dispenza

You Are the Placebo: Making Your Mind Matter – (Hay House 2014)

An invaluable book from a man who healed his broken back through his mind alone, and then spent thirty years researching and understanding the power of the mind to heal. Fascinating and full of scientific evidence on the power of placebos, which is written in easily understandable language.

Becoming Supernatural: How Common People Are Doing the Uncommon – (Hay House 2018)

> Dr Dispenza draws upon the latest research in neuroscience, epigenetics, neurocardiology, quantum physics and other scientific areas to show how human transformation and change take place and what it can mean for our lives. By reconditioning your body to a new mind, you can shift your awareness to new possibilities in the future. Full of practical exercises and clearly explained science.

MEGAN DEVINE

It's OK That You're Not OK – (Sounds True 2017)

> Having witnessed her forty-year-old partner drown in front of her eyes, Megan, a trained psychotherapist, rethought the whole way we deal with grief. This is one of the most moving and practical books I have read on how to go forward after tragedy.

EDITH EGER

The Choice – (Rider 2018)

> A remarkable and powerful Holocaust story. Although the first section of the book deals with Eger's life in Auschwitz, the rest of the book describes how she rebuilt her life after her experiences during the war, how she faced up to her demons and case studies of her work as a psychotherapist.

JEFF FOSTER

Falling in Love with Where You Are – (Non-Duality press – New Harbinger 2013)

> Having spent years dealing with depression and illness, Jeff embarked on a spiritual quest to discover the truths of existence. What he found was that 'healing doesn't always feel good' and from that premise, this book – through prose and poetry – guides the reader to understand that reaching 'home' can be

lonely and sometimes exhausting, but you can find calm in the middle of the storm.

The Way of Rest – (Sounds True 2016)

It is very hard to describe this book which is part poetry, part reflections and part a series of songs from the deep heart. Beautifully written and deeply insightful. it is a lesson on how to stop trying to work out everything in life and learning to accept life as it is.

The Deepest Acceptance – (Sounds True 2012)

A book full of insights into how the armour we wear protects us from the full experience of life and by stripping that away you can embrace life now and live in the moment.

VICTOR FRANKL

Man's Search for Meaning – (Rider new ed. 2004)

The seminal work of the internationally renowned psychiatrist. Written over fifty years ago it is still as powerful and relevant today as ever. A remarkable blend of science and humanism, at the core of which is the belief that man's primary motivational force is his search for meaning.

IAN GAWLER

Meditation Pure and Simple – (New Age Books 1996)

For those wanting a short introduction to the subject, this book makes sense of meditation and helps initiate you into its practice.

DANIEL GOLEMAN AND RICHARD DAVIDSON

The Science of Meditation: How to Change Your Brain, Mind and Body – (Penguin 2018)

A comprehensive and detailed scientific account of how meditation spread in the West and the benefits of its practice.

MINDY GREENSTEIN AND JIMMIE HOLLAND

Lighter as We Go: Virtues, Character Strengths and Aging – (Oxford University Press 2018)

Taking an intergenerational approach to how we age, this book is full of research and personal stories of what we fear as we age and how we learn who we are as we grow older.

LOUISE HAY

You Can Heal Your Life – (Hay House 1984)

Founder of the Hay House publishing house, Louise has written numerous books on the relationship between the mind and body and how you can heal your life and discover and implement the potential of your own creative powers for personal growth and self-healing. This book is full of her ideas and strategies to help you heal.

RABBI ABRAHAM JOSHUA HESCHEL

I Asked for Wonder – (Crossroad Publishing 2018)

A book full of Heschel's awe-inspiring insights into the ineffable nature of God and the universe.

The Sabbath – (Macmillan 1951)

A beautifully written book in Heschel's inimitable style about the beauty of Judaism's holiest day of the week. Combining the Sabbath laws with his insights into how we can understand them within a metaphysical framework.

ALEJANDRO JUNGER

Clean – (HarperOne 2012)

This book is subtitled 'The revolutionary program to restore the body's natural ability to heal itself' and that is what it is about. Based on the premise you are what you eat, it delves deeply into explaining the reasons so many problems arise because of our diet. It then details a complete detox programme.

ANNE KARPF

The War After: Living with the Holocaust – (Mandarin 1997)

A moving book that is part memoir and part historical and psychological research on the effects of being a child of Holocaust survivors.

DAVID KESSLER

Finding Meaning: The Sixth Stage of Grief – (Rider 2019)

The five accepted stages of grief are supplemented in this book by a sixth stage, which explains how finding meaning in loss can transform it into a more peaceful and hopeful experience. This book is a wonderfully informative and uplifting treatise on the nature of grief.

JACK KORNFIELD

The Art of Forgiveness, Lovingkindness and Peace – (Bantam Books 2008)

A beautiful short book that is full of wisdom and practical meditations that will bring you peace and comfort as you live through life's challenges.

MICHIO KUSHI

The Macrobiotic Way: The Definitive Guide to Macrobiotic Living – (Avery 2004)

This is the most comprehensive guide to macrobiotics from one of the leaders in the international macrobiotic community. It discusses not just macrobiotic food but the entire lifestyle that it encompasses and is filled with advice and recipes for curing a whole host of ailments.

ANITA MOORJANI

Dying to Be Me – (Hay House 2012)

This is an extraordinary account of a Near Death Experience (NDE) that transformed Anita's life in a miraculous way and taught her how to live now.

What If This Is Heaven – (Hay House 2016)

A follow-up to her previous book, this examines the common myths that hold us back in life, and how by freeing ourselves from these falsehoods, we can live lives of purpose and joy. Each chapter has exercises to guide the reader through how they can break up established myths to improve their wellbeing.

RICHARD E. NISBETT

The Geography of Thought: How Asians and Westerners Think Differently and Why – (Nicholas Brealey 2005)

A fascinating book about how the origin of different cultures in the West and the East developed different thought patterns and ways of seeing the world.

ELAINE NUSSBAUM

Recovery from Cancer – (SquareOne 2004)

A very touching, detailed account of one woman's cancer journey and how she beat the odds of survival by practising macrobiotics and healing therapies.

MELANIE REID

The World I Fell Out Of – (Fourth Estate 2019)

An incredibly honest and inspiring memoir by a journalist whose lifechanging accident left her wheelchair bound. As she tells the story of her struggles to recover as much mobility as she could, she reminds us that we need to appreciate the life and blessings we have, which must never be taken for granted.

RACHEL NAOMI REMEN

Kitchen Table Wisdom: Stories That Heal – (Riverhead Books 1996)

As one of the earliest pioneers in the mind-body health field and cofounder of the Commonweal cancer centre, Rachel Naomi Remen is more than just a doctor and counsellor. As a long-time survivor of serious chronic illness, she brings a unique perspective to healing suffering through finding meaning, love and hearing people's stories.

My Grandfather's Blessings: Stories of Strength, Refuge, and Belonging – (Riverhead Books 2000)

The granddaughter of an orthodox rabbi who taught her that blessing one another is what fills our emptiness, Rachel Naomi Remen shows how serving others heals us.

DON MIGUEL RUIZ

The Four Agreements – (Amber-Allen Publishing 1997)

Based on ancient Toltec wisdom, this book discusses the source of our self-limiting beliefs and offers ways to transform our lives to experience true freedom, happiness and love.

SOPHIE SABBAGE

The Cancer Whisperer: Finding Courage, Direction and the Unlikely Gifts of Cancer – (Coronet-Hodder & Stoughton 2015)

This book was the turning point in my cancer journey. It is the first book I recommend to anyone with cancer. It reframes cancer into something that can heal you, rather than you having to be healed from it. It is full of practical advice that helps you understand how you can help yourself to go forward, dealing with every aspect of cancer.

Lifeshocks: And How to Love Them – (Coronet – Hodder & Stoughton 2018)

A lifeshock is an unwanted and unexpected moment in our life. This book discusses the different type of lifeshocks through autobiographical accounts and shows how they can bring healing, transformation and peace.

RABBI LORD JONATHAN SACKS

Since completing this book, Rabbi Lord Jonathan Sacks tragically passed away. He was one of the world's foremost religious leaders and thinkers and has written a large number of books. Over the years I have managed to read many of them. They have helped to both broaden my horizons and sharpen my ideas about many things in Judaism and beyond. I have highlighted just two that I specifically refer to in this book.

To Heal a Fractured World: The Ethics of Responsibility – (Bloomsbury 2005)

With his unique perspective bringing together biblical narrative, kabbalah and ancient and modern philosophy, Rabbi Sacks argues the case for life being God's call to responsibility.

Morality: Restoring the Common Good in Divided Times –
(Hodder & Stoughton 2020)

> A further development of the ideas in the book above, focusing
> on how the loss of society's traditional values requires us, more
> than in any time in the past, to rebuild our common moral
> foundation.

OLIVER SACKS

The Man Who Mistook His Wife For a Hat (Picador 1986)

> One of the world's best-known neurologists describes numer-
> ous case studies of people whose memories and identities have
> been fractured and are no longer able to recognize themselves
> or others. A fascinating book about how broken minds can offer
> insights into the mystery of consciousness.

SHERYL SANDBERG

Option B: Facing Adversity, Building Resilience and Finding Joy –
(WH Allen 2017)

> A personal account of how Sandberg dealt with her husband's
> sudden death at the age of forty-four. Its thoughtful and hopeful
> message is enhanced by the practical guidance she gives on how
> we can build resilience in so many aspects of our lives.

DAVID SERVAN-SCHREIBER

Anti Cancer: A New Way of Life – (Penguin 2007)

> Together with the *Cancer Whisperer,* this is one of the key books
> to read if you want to heal yourself from cancer or prevent it
> from developing. Told through the story of his own cancer
> journey, this is a most thoroughly-researched book on how you
> can build your body's natural defences.

SMADAR SHIR

Miriam's Song – (Gefen 2016)

> A most tragic story of Miriam Peretz, a mother who lost two
> sons while they were serving in the Israeli army, and a husband
> who died of a broken heart. It is one of the most inspiring books

I have ever read. Peretz was awarded the Israel Prize for her courage and ongoing activities inspiring thousands of army recruits and school children all over the country.

Bernie Siegel

Peace, Love and Healing: The Path to Self-Healing – (Rider Books 1990)

This book was published over thirty years ago but became the forerunner of so many books that try to understand how mental attitudes can influence physical outcomes.

How to Be an Exceptional Patient – (Harper Books)

Another book which, thankfully, I read early on in my cancer journey. It helped me to understand the importance of taking responsibility for overseeing my own medical progress, dealing with doctors, treatments, etc. But more importantly, it helped me gain insight into how a positive attitude helps improve medical outcomes.

Rabbi Adin Even-Israel Steinsaltz

The Soul – (Maggid Books 2018)

As one of the preeminent sages of our generation, Rabbi Steinsaltz shows us how we can become sensitised to our souls opening new perspectives in our lives.

Rabbi Joseph B. Soloveitchik

Kol Dodi Dofek: Listen – My Beloved Knocks – (Ktav 2006)

In this book, Rabbi Soloveitchik discusses the existence of fate and the existence of destiny, and that by changing the question from why has this happened to what can I do with my suffering, he posits the answer lies in finding purpose. Taking this from an individual to a national level he extends this to destiny of the people of Israel in history.

HAEMIN SUNIM

The Things You Can See Only When You Slow Down – (Penguin 2018)

> A perfect, beautiful book to keep by your bedside. Full of short meaningful thoughts to contemplate at the end of a busy day.

ANDREW WEIL

Spontaneous Healing – (Warner Books 1995)

> This groundbreaking book affirmed Dr Weil's place as the foremost exponent of integrative medicine. So many of his ideas have now been confirmed by research and adopted around the world.

8 Weeks to Optimum Health – (Little Brown and Company 1997)

> A follow-up to *Spontaneous Healing,* this book takes many of the principles discussed in it and outlines an eight-week programme which shows how simple changes to your lifestyle can have long lasting effects.

CHRIS WOOLLAMS

The Rainbow Diet – and How It Can Help You Beat Cancer (Cancer Active 2008)

> A book that details the way diet can influence the prevention of cancer. The enormous amount of detailed information on so many foods and supplements can be a bit overwhelming and the style is somewhat sensationalist, but it is worth a read.

GARY ZUKAV

The Seat of the Soul – (Simon and Schuster 1989)

> With a scientist's eye and a philosopher's heart, Zukav takes you on a journey to the new way of looking at our souls as the seat of our intentions, motivations and interactions with others.